IS THIS REAL?

IS THIS REAL?

IS THIS REAL?

OUR STORY OF LIVING WITH SCHIZOPHRENIA

CAMERON AND TARA LEIPER

Cherish
EDITIONS

First published in Great Britain 2021 by Cherish Editions

Cherish Editions is a trading style of Shaw Callaghan Ltd & Shaw Callaghan 23 USA, INC.

The Foundation Centre

Navigation House, 48 Millgate, Newark

Nottinghamshire NG24 4TS UK

www.triggerpublishing.com

Text Copyright © Tara and Cameron Leiper

British Library Cataloguing in Publication Data

A CIP catalogue record for this book is available upon request from the British Library

ISBN: 9781913615130

This book is also available in eBook format:

ePUB: 9781913615147

Tara and Cameron Leiper have asserted their right under the Copyright, Design and

Patents Act 1988 to be identified as the authors of this work

Cover design by More Visual

Typeset by Lapiz Digital Services

ABOUT THE AUTHORS

Cameron Leiper is the second of four children. Schooled in Aberdeen, he now lives with his wife of twenty-six years in the village of Alford.

Tara is originally from Elgin and qualified as a classroom music teacher from the Northern College of Education and worked for more than a decade at Aberdeen College. She now runs an independent music teaching practice. She is active as an accompanist and vocal coach and is passionate about amateur and community music making.

They are married to one another and live together in the north east of Scotland.

CONTENTS

CHAPTER 1
INTRODUCTION

The Facts About Schizophrenia

At some point in their lives, 1 in 100 people will suffer from an episode of schizophrenia and 1 in 6 people will need treatment for mental ill health during their lifetime, according to livingwithschizophreniauk.org.

At any one time, 220 000 people are being treated for schizophrenia in the UK by the NHS. Mental health can and does affect thousands of people in the UK and impacts on the lives of individuals and their relationships.

I'm sure some people wonder what it's like to have schizophrenia. My answer is that, for me, it is an extremely frightening world. Every decision feels like life or death. Everything is upsetting, unforgiving and so harrowing.

I stood at the back door of the fish house. It was raining and I was the only person standing outside for my afternoon tea break. I was way, way too uncomfortable to even entertain having a cigarette with my fellow workers. My blue boiler suit and white T-shirt were already damp with all the spray, water and ice from working on the fish. The rain just made me colder. On an average day, I, like every other smoker at the fish house, took an extra break for a cigarette in the toilets. It was customary to sit on the toilet water tank with your feet resting on the bowl top, thus making it harder for the management to identify and harass you. Other times, I would often pass people in the hall, from lowly workers to the owner. I dealt with this situation by reciting the Shakespeare soliloquy from Macbeth, "Tomorrow, and tomorrow, and tomorrow, creeps in this petty pace from day to day." I thought people could read my mind, therefore I wanted people to think well of me. (1988)

Cameron and I have been married for twenty-five years. We have no children, just cats. Cameron was diagnosed with chronic paranoid schizophrenia in 1988 and has been unable to work since then. I am now a freelance music teacher, performer and conductor.

This book is not concerned with attempting to discover why mental illness has been thrust upon us or to assign blame, or to work out and explain what contributory factors came into play in the causing of a brain to malfunction. This book is not concerned with our biographies or life histories; we are not writing about childhood experiences and what we have done with our lives up until this point, although some past experiences will be referred to throughout these pages. Rather, this book hopes to tell the story of our lives together today, this week and this year. It will tell of our normal everyday activities and experiences from our breakfast routine to visiting friends, watching TV, playing golf and shopping. It will allow you some insight into what life is like for us on a day-to-day basis as we learn to live with mental illness. We accept that schizophrenia is part of our lives and here we make our meagre attempts to understand each other and hope that this contributes something useful to you, the reader.

I knew of Cameron's mental illness before we married in 1994. It did not faze me, and I was not worried for my own safety. In fact, the issue of safety has never entered my head. I just accepted that he had issues with his thinking and perceptions. I never really considered how this might impact our relationship then or in the future. I remember the evening he told me of his illness. The conversation was full of gaps and lengthy silences as I asked him to just spit out whatever he was trying to say. I do tend to say things as they are! It seemed to be an eternity of me reassuring him that things would be okay no matter what he had to say, and that he just had to form the words and let them out.

Eventually, he told me he suffered from schizophrenia. I knew it was a huge deal for him to tell me because of the protracted silences and inability to formulate words. I was expecting something really disastrous, but when I found out that it was a mental illness, I did wonder what all the fuss had been about.

Looking back, I was young and naïve and probably rather selfish. I hadn't really thought about how this illness was debilitating for Cameron or how it might affect our lives in the future. My life was fine, and his illness did not seem to negatively affect him in my eyes, so I did not think much more about the whole issue. Cameron was, perhaps, worried that I would think him a weirdo or that the idea of him being mentally ill might scare me off or stop me wanting to be with him. The truth is, had he never told me about being ill, I would not have been able to guess, in any way.

My first and enduring impressions of Cameron are of a tall, dark and handsome chap with really sad, beautiful eyes. Although a little shy, he is the most generous person I have ever met, with the most gentlemanly of manners. I am, of course, biased in my opinion! None of these traits have changed or diminished over time and he is always kind and thoughtful. Just because there may be chemical imbalances in your brain does not mean that you cannot also have a pleasant, kind and giving nature. He also has a witty, often childlike, sense of humour!

It is usually me who tells other people about Cameron suffering from schizophrenia, but this is probably because new acquaintances come through me rather than him. I asked Cameron how many people he had told about his illness and he said, "Not many." He is now not as worried about telling people, but initially he thought that people might not be friendly with him because the illness has a stigma attached to it. People may react according to prejudicial and stereotypical opinions, rather than getting to know him on his own merits.

As individuals, we each inhabit our own world within our bodies, and take it (or it takes us) into different situations and environments. We are living out our own unique lives inside ourselves, with our own thoughts, actions, experiences, preferences and opinions. With so many of us living around each other, but in our own worlds, it is a wonder that any sense of cooperation and community can be achieved at all when we each have our own priorities and agendas. Somehow, though, we succeed and learn how to live with each other.

We cannot become another person; we cannot even come close. We have no direct way of finding out what it is like to live the life of someone else. We sometimes hear of two people (or more) living so much in sync with one another that each can finish the other's sentence or know what the other is thinking. It is often recounted that twins have this ability, but this is less surprising given their biological beginnings.

So, with each of us leading our own way through life, it is encouraging to find others who seem alike in personality and interests – people we feel an affinity with. We feel that the things we have in common bring us together, so we are less alone in our own worlds and feel part of something beyond ourselves. We use the commonalities as a bridge between our two unique worlds.

We discover these commonalities through communicating with each other: talking, looking, feeling, writing, observing and listening. It is possible to connect with others as if we know them, even if we have never met, through various forms of media, written and spoken word, radio and television, music, film and documentary, art and literature. Through these, we can empathize with and imagine the lives of others, and this helps to bring us together by sharing experiences.

The obstacles of politics, race, class, belief, geography, affluence and time are all eroded as we are now able to access others' experiences readily in many formats. We become acquainted with historical figures, politicians, film and TV personalities, artists and sportspeople. We "get to know" composers, singers, athletes and others in our area of interest, as we read and watch and discuss. We spend time with them and their work and, as such, develop some kind of relationship with them. How (and why) these people are portrayed will affect our relationships with them.

So, we can be brought closer together as human beings living in our own worlds by sharing stories and experiences, as these may provide common ground for communication, dialogue and empathy. As we tell stories, they provide a momentary representation of an experience or memory. Continually revisiting a memory, opinion or experience may allow us to clarify what can be learned from scrutinising it. As we look again and again at an issue, we find that we learn more about our own unique world perspective and how it fits or jars with the bigger picture of human life and sense of community. We can develop a greater and deeper appreciation for our own lives, problems, difficulties and successes, and move forward better informed.

Working on this book has been a "getting to know us" experience. By probing issues that are part of our everyday lives and thinking about them, scrutinising and questioning, we have both learned more about ourselves and each other: how each of our lives interplays, interjects, interconnects and impacts the other. All close relationships have this intersection of lives like a Venn diagram:

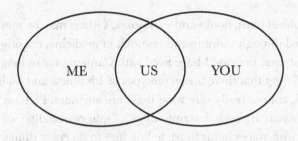

ME US YOU

As we have become more familiar with the issues of the other and questioned and reasoned things through, so the area of overlap between the circles has increased. "Our world" is larger and more solid than before, involving more of each of us coming together to create a growing and flourishing "us". Sharing experience is part of what it means to be human for many. As a result of getting to know us, we hope that you, the reader, will know yourself and your world more deeply and intimately.

Cameron and I have shared the writing of this book. Italics are used to denote Cameron's words and sometimes our initials, C and T, are used in a conversation so that the speaker is clear. When we are telling a shared tale, non-italicised font is used. Our story allows the outside world into our lives to glimpse what living with schizophrenia is like for us.

Our lives are unique and, as such, we would in no way suggest that ours is typical of anything at all. We do not claim to have answers or solutions to leading a better life if you are confronted with the challenge of living with mental illness and the problems encountered each day. We hope that in writing for, and about, ourselves, we may better understand each other and how to accommodate each other's needs and capabilities. The writing of this book allowed us to look afresh at problems, so we can negotiate each day a little more effectively than before.

It is impossible to discuss schizophrenia with a mind that is free from judgement or influence based on individual experience. What I mean is that we all have some idea in our head of what it might be like to have this mental illness. These initial perceptions may come from what we have heard in the news, fictitious and biographical films, books and even jokes. Others may be more informed through training and research in medicine, nursing or social care. Because I have lived with Cameron for so long, I often forget that there are stereotypes of his illness and, to be truthful, am not really sure what these are anymore. Perhaps the most obvious are such descriptions as a "split personality" or the lunatic with voices in his head, telling him to do crazy things. The "crazy" things that go on inside someone's head are not so crazy to the person experiencing them, and therein lies the whole story – trying to understand the thinking and behaviours that happen to each of us every day of our lives.

At some point in their life, one in one hundred people will suffer an episode of schizophrenia and one in six people will need treatment for mental ill health during their lifetime. At any one time, 220,000 people are being treated for schizophrenia in the UK by the NHS. Mental health can and does affect thousands of people in the UK and impacts on the lives of individuals and their relationships.

As I said, I often forget what the term means to those outside our personal lives, but occasionally there are cases on the news of atrocities committed by the mentally ill, or murder trials where a schizophrenia sufferer is the defendant. These reports jolt me into seeing how people with a mental illness are portrayed and how these cases can influence the judgement of members of the public. Such occasions make me become aware of the fear that might be associated with the term schizophrenia. It is not so long ago that those suffering these illnesses were persecuted and locked up in sanatoriums, forced to endure horrific treatments and left in isolation like caged animals.

Today, there are occasions when sufferers need to be sectioned as a precaution if it is deemed they are a danger to themselves and/ or others. I was recently reminded of the impact that the term schizophrenia can have upon others when I spent some time in discussion with my father, whom I do not see much due to his living abroad. He expressed concern for my safety, even after twenty years of marriage to Cameron. I was really taken aback as I had never thought that others had such thoughts about my relationship, as I felt so safe within it. I suppose that those who know me less might have thought that my safety could have been in jeopardy at times. I am delighted to say this has never been the case. If I was to describe Cameron in a word (or two), it would be a man of immense generosity, kindness and patience.

If anyone is "unstable" in our relationship, it would be me – the creative one! We do not often hear of the great generosity of spirit and kindness of those with a mental illness. Unfortunately, it is the "horror stories" that are relayed, rather than the heroic stories of living with a mental illness. I am very pleased to see broadcasting corporations running programmes of stories related to mental illness, as well as high-profile figures raising the issue of these unseen disabilities. There are many heroes battling life every day, both those suffering with a mental illness and those helping and supporting them as family, friends and carers. Online information is abundant, and we will include some helpful extracts from these throughout the text.

Why write a book?

I write this book so that sufferers of schizophrenia can hopefully have a glimmer of light at the end of the proverbial tunnel. When I became ill I had no idea what I was moving in to. It has been a massive learning curve. If you can see what might be coming, you can take appropriate measures to better remedy the situation. I write this book to give people an idea of what it is like to have this illness and to understand it a bit more. Although schizophrenics suffer intense and intrusive mental pain, and sometimes physical pain from such things as self-harm, everyone's suffering is unique. But pain is the constant. I hope, in this book, to be able to relieve the suffering of some individual, who, like me, didn't have a clue what was happening to them. A true friend would intervene with this, or another book – maybe read it to the affected person, or put into practice some ideas from the book. Do not leave your friend to suffer unchecked. An ill person's behaviour may be better understood by sharing my experiences with the world. You cannot see mental illness and I think it is important to raise awareness and understanding of what people endure so that we can all start talking more about this issue and realise that anyone we pass in the street may be a sufferer. I also hope that in writing this book it helps carers and family to better understand the difficult situation that we find ourselves in.

Recognising mental illness and telling others

I was admitted voluntarily to my local mental hospital in 1989, aged twenty-one. I was just going with the ebb and flow of the currents around me. I have a memory of my mum crying and my dad not doing so, as they drove away and left me behind. After about a fortnight, or thereabouts, I was in the smoking room one evening when one guy was asking everyone the same question, namely, "What are you in for?" When he asked me, I said that I didn't know. He kept probing with questions about the types of medication and dosage I was on. I realised then that one of my worst nightmares was about to become true. Minutes turned to hours and I could not see my psychiatrist soon enough to get some answers. I can't remember how long it was before I was seen, but trying to get the psychiatrist to say I had schizophrenia was like getting blood out of a stone. She was very reluctant to say it, in fact, presumably as a way of protecting me or preparing me for the terrible reality.

A new chapter of my life had begun. I could no longer draw strength from the fact that I was "normal". The next question was for how long had I been ill? Looking back now, I can see that I had certainly been ill for at least two years prior to being admitted to hospital. I was going around mentally ill for more than two years and no one told me. To be mentally ill, and not know it, is both frightening and disturbing. To think that I spent two years in psychosis unmedicated is probably going to be the most disturbing thing I will experience in my lifetime.

In the early 1990s, I had a few friends, so when I met Tara she had to be told everything. I told her as sensitively as I could because being mentally ill isn't the kind of thing you should keep private. She seemed okay with the news and I was very relieved. We seemed to have other things in common in our personal lives and I felt that the bonding between us was very strong because of this. This *made me happy. For one who had been so very lonely, this bonding was like an act of God.*

I remember the evening I had to tell Tara. I had two things to do: tell her about my illness and, hopefully for the last time, hide all my tablets. I had previously hidden all my medication away, because I did not want the risk of other people knowing about my illness. Not having to do so felt really good. I no longer felt I was alone as I had an army of two, for which I continue to feel blessed. Feelings of extreme euphoria replaced years of darkness and pessimism – the darkness and putrefying illness was a tunnel without light and no hope. Anything that, in any way, diverts you from such a blackness is divine. The intensity of the psychosis I suffered would destroy any man. This is where family is so important as they try to understand what you are dealing with. It is more than twenty-five years to the day since I told Tara and she is still here – hooray!

When it comes to telling other people about my illness, I am very guarded because I don't think the news will be received well. I think that some people might be more accepting and understanding than others. I leave Tara to let people know about my schizophrenia because I feel more secure that she will explain my situation well.

When I read Cameron's words, here, I am struck by the intensity and emotion behind them. Expressing anything, for Cameron, is very difficult, but it gives me courage to see some positivity in what he says. The following chapters contain darkness and disturbing concepts, but it is important to remember that there is some happiness and joy, even if it is transitory.

Although Cameron's illness has the label "schizophrenia", there are no two people who have the same symptoms, experiences or daily challenges. Being ill, as many know, is more than being the "label", and often the label itself can limit understanding and forward progression in life. The label can provide the sufferer with a starting point on their journey with coping. However, for the outsider looking in, a label may discourage dialogue or even set it off in a wrong direction. Sometimes people are too embarrassed, do not want to invade privacy or simply don't know how to have a conversation about mental illness. I was certainly ignorant of just how debilitating this illness is for Cameron until we started our writing collaboration. I was obviously aware of many issues that made his life difficult, but did not really understand *why*. My eyes have since been opened and we both hope you benefit from any insights this book may provide.

CHAPTER 2
BEING ME, INSIDE MY HEAD

The NHS website describes schizophrenia as a long-term severe mental illness that can cause a range of psychological symptoms. It is not a term used to describe someone who is violent and nor does it denote a person with a split personality. It continues to say that doctors describe this illness as a type of psychosis, which means that the sufferer may not be able to disentangle reality from their own distorted thoughts. The symptoms of schizophrenia include hearing or seeing things in your head (hallucinations), having unusual beliefs that are not based on reality (delusions) and muddled thoughts due to these two symptoms. In addition, many sufferers also lose interest in daily activities, stop looking after their personal hygiene and often avoid meeting people.

Another website we have found helpful in describing the symptoms of schizophrenia (see the Useful Webpages section at the end) is "Living with Schizophrenia". It clarifies the meaning of the two groups of symptoms that may be encountered – positive and negative. "Positive symptoms" is the term used to describe new thoughts or ways of doing things that were not there before the onset of the illness. This includes experiencing hallucinations or delusions. "Negative symptoms" is the label given to aspects of the sufferer's life that have stopped since becoming ill and this might include things like not socialising nor looking after themselves. The webpage continues by saying that someone with schizophrenia may have negative and positive symptoms and the severity of these will vary with each individual. I found it very surprising to read that symptoms can vary day to day or even hour by hour, and can also be weather and season dependent, with more admissions to psychiatric wards in the hot summer months. It also states that many people with this illness suffer "episodes" of being unwell. Unfortunately, Cameron suffers from chronic paranoid schizophrenia and experiences this all day, every day.

The Living with Schizophrenia site also gives examples of "odd" behaviour that may be observed in a suffering friend or family member, and states that although behaviour may be odd, the actions will make perfect sense inside the head of the sufferer, such as having to wear only clothes of a certain colour because they have been told to do so by voices in their mind.

I used to be very confused by the terms "positive" and "negative" in terms of symptoms of schizophrenia. I would have thought that all symptoms of a mental illness were negative, in that you do not want to have them. Indeed, they are something you are experiencing that you wish was not there. Likewise, the term "positive" implies something that is uplifting and makes you feel good – and I could not understand how experiencing hallucinations made you feel good. These are unfortunate labels to grapple with as a layperson. I find it easier to explain these to myself by thinking in terms of arithmetic: positive is a plus sign and it means you have gained something that was not there before; negative is a minus sign and it means that you are losing something, so you have less of a thing than you had before the onset of the illness. Psychotic thoughts are in the group of positive symptoms as they are something experienced now and were not there before the onset of illness.

Cameron has chronic paranoid schizophrenia. This means he does not have episodes of illness but is unwell all the time. There may be times of excessive stress when symptoms are heightened, but in general terms, Cameron is stable in his illness as he suffers the same levels of psychosis, delusions and negative symptoms all the time. I notice no change in his levels over the seasons.

From the first of the two reports included above, the line that I find most disturbing is "the person may not always be able to distinguish their own thoughts and ideas from reality". As mentioned in the introduction, we all inhabit our bodies, which take us through experiences and interactions with others. There is an assumption that an experience shared has elements in common for those experiencing it, but this is less likely when you are not in the same reality as others. Cameron often has different perspectives and assumptions concerning activities or social tasks we undertake, but I had not really considered the full extent that his positive symptoms have on these differences we experience. For example, after having a family meal, as we travel home in the car, Cameron will say that he didn't think the event went well at all, and frequently I may disagree with him. My perspective of how things went, their success or failure, is based on quite different criteria to his. If there was flowing conversation, a positive atmosphere, some laughing, then I think it was successful. Cameron will have been so absorbed in trying to muster his strength to deal with his "fault" thinking, that he was unaware of the successes outside of himself due to being so inwardly concentrated.

Psychotic thoughts and mind-reading

I am totally submerged in psychosis, a sea of psychosis. As a child, I used to wonder what it would be like inside the brain of a madman. The reality for me, today, is that it is an extremely overpowering, traumatising and deeply frightening place.

Looking back, I can now see when the onset of schizophrenia began. The illness at ten per cent of its strength, for me, takes everything I've got to deal with it. At one hundred per cent strength, psychosis is an unbearable existence, like being possessed. I was severely ill for at least two years before I got any help. I was working full-time in a fish filleting factory and, of course, was unmedicated. Everyone knew I was ill, but I didn't – which, looking back, is most disturbing. To give an example: when I slipped into full psychosis mode, I very slowly turned my head in a possessed fashion, knife in hand from my factory piecework, with voices in my head telling me to kill. All my attention, thoughts and feelings were focused on a man working near me. On top of this, I thought that the work radio was controlling my thoughts and behaviours because I believed each line of every song was talking about me and this made me feel really bad. My fellow workman was very uncomfortable as I gazed at him. My head was full of murderous and violent thoughts. The voices in my head continued with the word "kill". It is even sadder when you factor in that he was one of the nicest men in the entire factory. He was a good, funny, warm-hearted man – a real gentleman.

It is quite unbelievable and yet fortunate that nothing awful happened during those two years when I had no medication, no friends, no counselling and no safety net. The warning signs were everywhere but being ill for the first time, I didn't see the illness creeping up and taking control.

It was recently brought to my attention that nobody realises they are ill with psychosis the first time it happens. My heart really goes out to them because I know nothing is so disturbing and shocking. It has been decades since I first became ill without medication and I don't like thinking about it much, because I still find it all too much.

As well as being so upsetting, those premedication years were so, so lonely, completely without hope, with no light at the end of the tunnel. I continued in deep despair day after day, year after year. My family environment was so dysfunctional that I could not live at home. I was living in a static caravan with no heating. I remember snowdrifts outside and all I had to combat that was a so-called thermal top. I was sitting in my living room absolutely freezing and shivering and so lonely. At that point, my sadness was complete.

I'm increasingly beginning to think my very traumatic childhood was priming me for a very traumatic adulthood. When, as a child, I did little else but worry profusely and became traumatised, these became learned behaviours. As a child, I thought that worrying was an adult trait and to be encouraged as it was "mature". As an adult, I know that steps should be taken to minimise worry. The learned behaviours from childhood just continued and became the norm as I knew nothing different.

Before being referred to the medical services, I was, and still am, suffering from something known as "ideas of reference". Put simply, if, for example, the radio DJ was talking, I would think he and the message had special significance and importance for me. This was the same with a television presenter or song, or a mundane conversation — the emotions and gut feelings I experienced would be based upon the content of what I was hearing. You feel extremely possessed. I think the word "possessed" is very apt. If someone came on the television and was reporting on a successful businessman, I would sit there smiling and feeling very pleased with myself, thinking they were referring to me. Equally, if a heinous crime is being reported, then I will have a gut reaction of guilt and feel really, really bad, almost physically sick. I understand "ideas of reference", how it works and that my emotions are being hijacked. I cannot rely on my reactions *because I know they have been altered and influenced. They are not a true reflection of how I want them to be because I am not in control of them. I still suffer from these ideas today, but am glad the scale is quite diminished. These days, I can see more objectively what is happening, that I am being controlled and am aware of the influence upon me. However, even though the problem is part diminished with the help of medication, you need to relearn behaviours, social conventions and manners, as best you can.*

Wikipedia describes "ideas of reference" as when a person experiences coincidences and assigns personal meaning to them. This is part of the diagnostic criteria in many psychotic mental illnesses, including paranoid schizophrenia. The "Better Help" website describes ideas of reference as false beliefs that random coincidences in the world directly relate to the sufferer, as either the cause of them or that they were designed specifically for them. It goes on to say that there are many different kinds of "distorted thinking'" that can be observed, such as black and white thinking or believing things that align with your own beliefs and discounting others, blaming bad things on external forces and taking the credit for good things. These can be considered delusional when the sufferer is certain they are true, they cannot be persuaded it is false and the delusion is not capable of being true.

I've had this illness for 30 years now. Not long after I was diagnosed with chronic paranoid schizophrenia, my parents took me out to lunch to a trendy seaside café. I was completely overwhelmed with terror and could not have been more frightened. I felt controlled by the background conversations, and if I spoke, it wasn't to my parents, but to the main voice from the background chatter. The illness was vicious in its ferocity. I had feelings of being possessed, people controlling me with their conversation. I thought they could all read my mind. For years and years, this was the norm for me. Without fail, the trauma was immeasurable every single time. When working in the factory at the time of the onset of my illness, I believed that people could read my mind effortlessly. I used to try and recite sections of Shakespeare's plays in my head, so that if my thoughts were read, people would think I was intelligent. Even today, I still think that people can read my mind.

When outside, I usually try to get things done as fast as possible. The longer I am outside, the more ill I feel. I usually try so hard to be quick that I end up looking a bit unconventional. This stresses me a lot. For example, if I see a man walking with his child, I am immediately fighting psychotic thoughts. I usually lose. I think the man can read my mind by looking where I'm looking and following the exact direction my eyes take. He can see the psychotic thoughts I'm having about him or his child, or both. I feel I'm going to be seriously harmed because of these thoughts. This repetitive loop happens each time I pass someone in the street. This is one of the reasons I do not wish to go outside. The trauma you go through for one fight against odd thoughts is incredible. To have it repeating in a loop fashion is unimaginable.

T   What do you mean by "the more ill I feel" when you are outside and looking "unconventional"?

C   I will get more bad thoughts than normal, an amplification of the problem and more intensity to the thoughts. I am unconventional-looking because of the speed that I am going about my business. Everyone else is moving at four miles per hour and I am moving at six miles per hour and cutting in on people.

T   Do other people not also walk fast?

C   Not as fast as me.

T   So, I have lived with you for decades and cannot say you walk quickly – in fact, I think you walk slowly. So why would you think you are drawing attention from going quickly, when you are not? Could it be that your "mind" is racing and so it transfers to your body in kind? In other words, not actually moving quickly, but thinking it is moving quickly due to the urgent need to get home to safety.

C   Cutting in on people means I must be going quickly, like in the supermarket aisles. There is a little junction where you go down one aisle or the other – I normally come out of an aisle and go left and just cut off others.

T   Do you not think this is normal behaviour in the

C   supermarket as everyone has a trolley and is trying to get stuff done?

C   Mm. Maybe.

T   My perceptions are that you are not quick and do not move in an unconventional way in the supermarket or in the street. I know you may think you are, but from my observation you are not. Does that make you feel any better?

C   I suppose it does. But I do get funny looks when going round with my trolley.

T   Many people may look at each of us funnily for different reasons. Perhaps the mood they are in, or someone just happens to catch your eye. It does not mean it has to be because of your behaviour.

C   They are looking where I'm looking…

T   You think the man looks at your eyes, follows your eyes and then can read your mind. How? I don't understand. Do you think everyone can read minds?

C   Yes, in some form or another, I would say everyone can read minds. How is it done? Well, the person follows my eyes from item to item or person to person and condenses the different images into one.

T   You are assuming that the person looking at you sees the objects or people you are looking at and then combines them together in the way that your mind did. Surely there are many ways of putting two random objects or people together in a thought – one of them being that there is no link whatsoever between the object or person.

C   I agree that in an ideal world that may be the case.

T   I am trying to show you that there is more than one way to combine images (one being non-combining) and that not everyone is likely to put things together in the same way as you from two random objects that might catch your eye. You think because it is that way for you, it is that way for everyone else?

C	Yeah, maybe.
T	But can you see that it may not be that way for others?
C	It may not be that way for others, but the ability to make the link is still there.
T	Do you think I can read minds in the way you are describing?
C	Mm, if you wanted to.
T	What do you mean "if I wanted to"?
C	If you needed to or wanted to.
T	Why would I need to or want to?
C	I don't know – stress?
T	Do you think I can read your mind?
C	Probably, yeah.
T	In the same way you described above?
C	Yeah.
T	I have never read your mind. I do not know how to read your mind. I cannot read your mind. What do you say to that?
C	It gives me a little bit of hope.
T	Do you believe what I said is the truth?
C	Yes.
T	Do you think I am typical of humanity in terms of biological and conceptual ability?
C	Oh yes.
T	So if I have never read your mind, it is likely that others have not, yes?
C	Okay.
T	Is it likely that I am the only person who does not have the ability to read minds?
C	No, not very likely.
T	Does that make you feel a bit better?
C	I suppose it does, yeah.
T	So, you do not have proof of others reading your mind? Perhaps you are just anxious about the possibility that someone could read your mind if it were possible?
C	Maybe.

I had no idea that Cameron thought all his thoughts were being seen by everyone he made contact with, including me. This would explain the safety fears he experiences when out and about – he is under the impression that people see his disturbing thoughts, too, and therefore he expects to be treated badly as punishment for having these images in his head. Each person Cameron passes is threatening in that they may be able to read his mind and punish him for what is "seen". It encourages me a little that Cameron can recognise that if I cannot read minds, then it is likely that most other people cannot either. Even if this "fact" is understood objectively by Cameron, it is also understandable that the possible threat of even one person demonstrating this ability would be enough to jeopardise his safety. Just because a statement is made negating the possibility of mind-reading does not really help to alleviate the feelings of anxiety for one's safety. The conceptual brain and the limbic system of fight or flight do not always concur and work harmoniously. You can know the fact, but the emotions can still be overwhelming.

When people talk, I think they are talking about me. I sometimes know what is happening and although I say to myself that they are not talking about me, I am afraid my gut emotion tells me otherwise. In other words, I feel the emotion carved by their words and this leaves me open to manipulation. When at home, I feel that people driving past my house can read my mind. I feel that they look through the holes in the hedge and see my body language in relation to engine revs. They can fathom my thoughts by the way I move and respond to these noises. When outside, I become affected by the loudness of the traffic; the louder the traffic noise, the more upset I become. The louder the traffic noise, the more put down I feel.

    Having really bad intrusive thoughts about loved ones, family and friends, without exception, should be seen by the sufferer as random brain activity. As well as these thoughts being random brain activity, I give little weighting of importance in any way to these completely random thoughts. I was surprised recently to learn that obsessive compulsive disorder (OCD) can cause thoughts of a blasphemous nature. I hope this brings you, the sufferer, some comfort, as it gave me a great deal of relief. It seemed like a weight had been lifted from my shoulders and I felt much better about my psyche. Prior to this, there were times when I wondered if I was beginning to become evil.

When out and about, I suffer continuous and repetitive obsessive thoughts, which are very unpleasant in nature. I have decided that being mentally ill means my thoughts are sometimes "mentally ill". For a few years now, I have started trying to substitute obsessive thoughts in favour of positive thoughts. There is no point in giving up. I see positivity as a main tool to seriously dilute schizophrenia and begin to topple it. If, like me, you sometimes have difficulty getting rid of thoughts, my current strategy is to fill your head with positive thoughts as much as you can muster, then it won't matter as much and it will lessen the strain. It may even lead to a moment of happiness. I think about buying someone a present; what would I get them to make them feel happy? The time it takes to think about what to purchase and why is a successful distraction. It is how we deal with what goes through our heads that is important, and being able to do so with apt and appropriate weighting.

I used to give far too much weighting to randomised thoughts. I sometimes deem these as background radiation. This illness has to be fought your entire life. You must never roll over and die. It is a very dark road. There is no point in going there. You must continually keep chipping away. Most people are fighting for survival, one way or another, such as providing food on the table and a roof over their heads, one day at a time. Has it ever been easy? Be very determined and remember you are looking for long-term success. There are certainly no quick fixes. Fight for how you want to be. A determined fighting spirit will genuinely take you a long way. It has taken me a long time to learn this.

Cameron refers to his psychotic thoughts as odd thoughts. Throughout these pages, he refers to them and how debilitating they are. I realise how daunting the prospect is to have to linger on one of these thoughts, but I asked him if he could explore one to share here to help the reader better understand. The thoughts may be fleeting, or on a loop, but the strategy is to avoid them and to distract the mind away from them. He bravely agreed to try and put into words the abstract experience of a psychotic thought and its impact.

Most of my psychotic thoughts are violent. Often, these thoughts involve an image of something to which a pane of glass is automatically placed in front of. The windowpane is then smashed, leaving a trail of blood and lethal shards of glass. This is the most common of ill thoughts I have. Often with psychotic thoughts, there is a distinct element of spontaneous urge to make things twice as awful. This could be, for example, willing some broken glass into someone's face, or lunging at someone passing by with garden shears, or getting a spontaneous urge to swerve the steering wheel toward an oncoming car. These urges sometimes make me feel physically sick.

One day, trying to cross the road, I was struggling. I could not focus on what I needed to do. Look one way, hold the image in my head, look the other way and then calculate when to cross. Halfway across the road, I had an image of me being smashed by a car. Whenever I let an image form in my mind, it goes psychotic without fail. I never consciously let an image form in my mind because I am trying to halt the psychosis. So, how do you cross the road if you can't hold an image in your mind? This is the simplest of tasks, which can be extremely dangerous for me.

I still, today, hear voices in my head. It used to be a lot worse. I find the voice usually kicks in when walking away from someone, such as the till operator in a shop. I hear a disgusting commentary, highly insulting, extremely crude, at which point you just disintegrate. Other types of voice I hear is the word "kill". It is not so bad these days, but it is triggered when I push my brain for more. I have learned to live with these problems. The most frequent psychotic thought I have involves spontaneously seeing a weapon of death from a mundane object. Anything that has corners, I see as a weapon for inflicting physical mutilation. For example, the corner of a photo frame could be treated as though it were an axe. Similarly, anything with a point could be interpreted as a kind of knife for stabbing. These thoughts are completely spontaneous in nature and take up a large part of my thinking.

When holding a real knife, I feel very uncomfortable – definitely ill at ease. It is obviously a dangerous weapon and my unease probably goes back thirty years to when I was a fish filleter, hearing the voice "kill" inside my head, working all day with a lethal knife and immersed in a wild sea of psychosis. In these mundane objects I identify as a weapon, as soon as I perceive that it is a weapon, I start back-pedalling immediately, trying not to have an image of this weapon in use. I am trying desperately not to have an image of mutilation in my head. The draw and power of psychosis is immense, like a strong magnet pulling you in. I don't want intrusive psychotic images, so I allow no images to form in my mind as a way to stop the flow of psychosis.

These quick, spontaneous, odd, ill thoughts do not last long. Perceiving the weapon in the first second, then trying to halt the formation of the mental imagery would take between one and five seconds, depending on the success of my attempts.

When trying to fend off a loop of psychotic thoughts, trying to stop the combining imagery in mutilation, my mind is stuck in focusing on two objects. For example, my feet moving forward and some poor victim's face. These are the only two thoughts I have, so over and over again I am trying not to combine the same two images. When presented with this psychotic loop, you must try to neutralise the thought. I am fending off the imagery many times but never wholly successfully. It is very draining. Things can go exponentially wrong in this kind of situation. Things easily get out of hand and it feels like life or death. Rapid escalation can quickly occur. There is nowhere I can look to stop the psychotic thoughts. If I focus on any object, it becomes psychotic and then everything becomes a damage limitation exercise. It is so degrading. The percentages and kinds of psychotic thoughts I experience are a) mutilation (80 per cent), b) sexual (10 per cent), c) evil (5 per cent) and d) perverse (5 per cent).

T   Do you see these thoughts as pictures, like a movie?

C   No, I try not to generate images in my head.

T   So are your psychotic thoughts word combinations?

C   No, they are images, like a photograph, but not fully formed. They are fleeting but disturbing.

T   Inside your mind's eye, do you "see" the bad event happening?

C   When my thoughts fail me, yes.

T   So, how often do your thoughts fail you, in that you do "see" the bad event happen?

C   About a quarter of my battles with psychotic thoughts fail me.

T   Are you anticipating a psychotic thought? Before a thought manifests itself, are you already fighting it?

C   No. It is only when there is a thought there, I think.

T   Do you have psychotic thoughts if you are sitting in a quiet place with your eyes shut and stimulus is removed?

C   The number of thoughts is diminished a lot, yes.

T   Would you still experience them, though?

C   Once I start thinking about something, that is when it all goes wrong.

T   Meditation and breathing exercises might be helpful as you focus on the sound and timing of your breath, and it allows the mind to become calm and "empty". What about wearing sunglasses or a peaked cap so your eyes are hidden?

C   I have thought about this, but I am scared it will draw attention towards me.

Outside, I also assume people can read my mind in relation to all the wrongs I have done before. I feel very worthless and ashamed. I feel that I am read like a book and also that sometimes I genuinely do not know if I am endangering myself through my behaviour. I don't know if I come across as normal or not. I don't know what percentage of other people's thoughts are failed thoughts like mine, where they are unable to clear a thought or image. The odd thoughts I experience have no bias in relation to the victim, be it man, woman, or child, but I find them most disturbing when involving children.

*   Let's assume I am in town, going about my business and trying not to upset pedestrians. A father and daughter are walking towards me. I would probably look towards the ground to avoid eye contact. I try everything to avoid any kind of contact or relationship being developed. I try to keep them as far away from me as possible, maintaining physical and mental distance. The further away I am from people allows me a sense of security. I find myself fighting thoughts of harming one or both these people (mutilative) and am extremely worried the father can read my mind. I am trying, flat out, to keep apace of these damned thoughts, unsure if I am going to come to some harm. It is not unusual for me to expect physical harm when passing someone. How many people do you pass on a pavement? This trauma repeats hundreds of times in the space of minutes. It must be detrimental to your mental state. While this is happening, I am also usually rigid with fear to the point that I am physically wrenched, making it even more difficult to deal with. I don't mind being put out too much, but it would be nice to be able to choose NOT to have these thoughts.*

T   How many times has someone lashed out at you in the last thirty years because of your psychotic thoughts? How many times have you been involved in a fight in that time?

C   None.

T   So, you want to take comfort from the fact that although you have experienced these thoughts and worried about them, there has never been an incident. You could maybe allow past experience to alleviate some of your anxiety about this: if it hasn't happened in the last thirty years, it is unlikely to start now.

C   I suppose so.

T   I realise you still have the same feelings of fear and of being "discovered", but the past dictates that this will not happen.

C   But there is no logic in madness. Somethings just do not make sense. That is why it is so difficult to understand.

T   But remembering that you have remained safe all these years may help a little. Learning from the past is useful and could act like a shield for you.

Safety

On a day-to-day basis, my head is a very frightening place, even though I still appreciate a bright morning and another fresh day. I'm convinced on all levels that something dreadful is going to happen to me, all day, every day – something truly terrible. I always feel that my neighbours, or anyone within my vicinity, are against me. This varies in degree dependent upon who it is that is near.

It is only the things that go through the mind that make a schizophrenic a schizophrenic. My head is always full of junk, a pile of rubbish not worth thinking about. I feel very strongly that the wiring inside my head is all wrong. That, to me, means getting a very wrong or highly inappropriate response all the time from my brain. This occurs at all levels of brain function. An absolute must for non-schizophrenics must be to retain the ability to "get rid of thoughts" when you want them to go. Me, I limp around not being able to dispose of highly psychotic thoughts, which only brings badness my way. This inability to clear the slate is so dangerous, on any level. I only see danger to myself. There's no way I could act on these thoughts and endanger another person. Like most people with mental illness that I've come into contact with, the 99.9 per cent of them are nice people, even with their problems. I can only think of one person whom I would categorise as dangerous in the nearly thirty years of contact with mental hospitals.

T   I am confused by what you mean by getting a highly inappropriate response as standard in relation to the wiring in your head. Can you explain it further?

C   It is like I have three terminals in my head: A, B and C. A should go to B and B should go to C. But in my head, when the message leaves A, it does not go to B. Instead, it travels off in the wrong direction and goes where it shouldn't.

T   So, you mean that your response to other people ends up being not what you intend. Therefore, the response is inappropriate in that you wished it to be something else entirely?

C   Yes, very much different.

T   Are you talking about responding in terms of eye contact, vocabulary choice, tone of the verbal response or body language? Or is it something else?

C   (Thoughtful.)

T   Is it only a thinking response you have to others? In other words, it is not necessarily externalised in word or action?

C   Correct. I must make my thought response look normal without lying.

T   And what about when you say it affects all levels of brain function. What do you mean by that?

C   For example, if I must do a sum in my head, the numbers themselves have a negative association. So instead of working on the sum itself, I am having to work on clearing the associated, negative thoughts connected with the numbers. I always come up with an uncomfortable answer, so I am not at peace with myself because these negative thoughts upset me.

T   Are you able to say in a clearer way what these inappropriate thoughts are?

C   A long time ago, I was on a bus and trying to read a book until my stop came, but I kept having psychotic thoughts – my brain, my book and a pedestrian's head all converge. So, those three elements come together to create a mutilative thought. Ninety per cent of my psychotic thoughts are mutilative in nature.

T   So, just to get this clear, when you talk about inappropriate responses, bad thoughts or psychotic thoughts, you are referring to your inability to control how you perceive objects and actions in the external world, and how your brain processes what is seen and thought about them. The result in your head or thinking is one that cannot be controlled, and it is upsetting to you because it concerns harm or mutilation happening to others?

C   Yes.

T   And this is why you feel unsafe?

C   Yes.

I don't feel safe at all when outside. My safety issues even plague me when I'm at home, making me very upset. Outside, I feel as if I'm going to get into a fight. I have such low self-esteem and self-confidence that I behave in a way that attracts people's disgust. I'd be as well drawing a large bull's eye on my back and waiting for all the arrows – believe me; they come in thick and fast. It's amazing how shamefully I've been treated in the past and what is yet to come? I put this down to the incorrect wiring in my head. I feel as though my brain is sending signals to the wrong part of my brain and there it is – a highly inappropriate thought. I don't trust my thinking.

T   When you say you feel as though you are going to be in a fight, does that mean you want a fight?

C   No. I feel that I am going to get battered by anybody – a yob, a bad person, someone looking for trouble. I reinforce that it is okay for other people to treat me badly. And it doesn't take long before they do.

T   What is it you do that makes you think you allow them to do this?

C   I am very dismissive of myself, showing that I have no self-worth and stuff like that.

T   You think they can tell this – how?

C   By what I say and how I speak to them.

T   So, that concerns people you are interacting with verbally. What about people you don't speak to?

C   My body language usually sets me up for a fall. I might have odd thoughts about my feet and this is frighteningly bad.

T   Not everyone is an expert in reading body language. Perhaps you think your body is giving out stronger signals because your head thinks it is?

C   Maybe.

T   What else can you say about the bull's eye comment and about arrows coming in thick and fast.

C   Once people start putting you down, they don't relent.

T   How do people put you down?

C   Do you remember that woman at the checkout the other day? They treat you with contempt, they're brash, they ridicule you, they are abrupt.

T   Could you consider her, simply, as a rude individual, as opposed to her behaviour being a direct result of your perceived negative influence upon her?

C   (Silence.)

T   So you think that your thoughts and body language make people act and react in a negative way, because of your effect on them? Are you able to change your body language so that it encourages positive behaviours from others instead of negative ones? Is that something you try to do?

C   Not really, no.

T   Why not? Would it perhaps make your life better?

C   Probably would, yeah.

T   So, is it worth trying to do that?

C   Yes, maybe. Well, I do try, in a roundabout way, I do try.

Concerning the passage about odd thoughts being the result of faulty wiring inside the brain, we had the following discussion:

T   Does it make you feel better or worse that the odd thoughts are out of your hands and out of your control, because it is due to the biology and chemistry of how the brain works?

C   Well, yes. I can't do anything about it.

T   I think, probably, what I was asking was does it make you feel better because you are then blameless for the thoughts?

C   No, I wouldn't consider myself blameless.

T   So, you can control the wiring in your brain?

C   No, you can't, not just by thinking about it.

T   Does that not make you blameless?

C   Maybe I am blameless, but other people wouldn't see it that way. They just think, "Here comes that nutter."

T   And what do you mean by "I don't trust my thinking", which you wrote at the end of the paragraph.

C   Getting inappropriate feedback from my brain.

T   Do you mean you cannot rely on your brain to do what you want it to do?

C   Yeah, at times, yeah.

Motivation

The "Living with Schizophrenia" website states that lack of motivation to do things for yourself, or to socialise, or even to express yourself is part of the negative symptoms of schizophrenia and can often be observed in the sufferer by friends and family members. These negative symptoms do not respond to anti-psychotic drugs and some medications may even cause side effects that are similar, such as lethargy.

Lack of motivation is a negative symptom of schizophrenia. Negative means that there is less of it than there was before. Some sufferers may experience a loss of interest in maintaining personal hygiene or in communicating, for example. For Cameron, a lack of motivation is a strong and debilitating symptom.

My schizophrenia affects me in many ways. The biggest problem is motivation; I have no motivation to look after myself properly; no motivation to do anything. I don't even have motivation to enjoy myself. Motivation to do anything has been gone for a long, long time. Important things don't get done. I rely heavily on Tara to do this for me. I rely on Tara for my meals, my clean clothes and cleaning the house. She has more to do as a result of my problems, which makes me feel bad. Sometimes, I feel so helpless. Some people think I'm lazy, but they don't know all the facts. When deciding whether to do something, my initial thought is how much my illness is going to upset me doing it. Harrowing situations are very commonplace for me living with my illness. This plays a very large part in determining whether I do or do not do something. To be honest, all things are harrowing, upsetting and humiliating. I am on the receiving end of all things degrading.

T   So, you feel that you would like to have some
      motivation – why?
C   Because more things would get done.
T   Like what?
C   Everything.
T   What specifically would you like to get done if you had the
      motivation to do it?
C   Cleaning, gardening…
T   But these things get done by me, so why do you need to do
      them?
C   To take the load off you.
T   Is your concern about lack of motivation linked to your
      guilt about me having to do things that would otherwise be
      done by you?
C   Yes, probably.
T   Do you have other issues related to lack of motivation?
      Why does it concern you so much that you are not
      motivated? In other words, is your main concern the
      inability to do your share of the household chores?

C	Yes.
T	What exactly do you mean by not being motivated?
C	I have no drive, no determination.
T	Do you think motivation is needed by people in order to successfully get through each day?
C	Yeah.
T	Why?
C	Because things will get done sooner rather than later.
T	When I do household jobs, do you think I was compelled to do them by motivation?
C	Maybe not.
T	So how did I manage to get them done if they were not dependent upon motivation? Are we confusing different kinds of motivation? You seem to be using lack of motivation for your inability to do things, is that correct?
C	Aye.
T	Are there differences between being motivated and simply getting on and doing what needs to be done? Is there a link?
C	Maybe not. But if you are not motivated, then you are not going to be enthusiastic about what you are doing.
T	Do you think I am enthusiastic about doing the household chores?!
C	More than I am! (Laughing.)
T	Maybe you are using lack of motivation as a reason for inactivity, but perhaps there are other reasons impacting on this rather than just motivation? Perhaps there are other reasons why you find it difficult to do things? You feel you have a lack of wanting to do things. Well, so do I, just not as much as you! You wrote that there is a definite link between you doing things and their negative impact on your thoughts. Is this not the reason that you do not want to do things? Is it a form of self-preservation?
C	The more I am forced to do, the more progressively ill I become. So, by not doing things, it is easier for me to maintain the status quo of my thoughts. The reason I

don't want to do things is because I want to cut down on the number of psychotic thoughts I have to deal with. It also means I am not exposing others to my illness, thereby protecting them from its impact.

T   So lack of motivation and the inability to want to do things is actually a result of self-preservation and a way of looking after yourself and others. Surely that is something to be encouraged. At the same time, we do need to learn how to live in the world and learn coping strategies for how to get through each day, because you can't get through life doing nothing.

C   I agree.

My medication totally kills me off in terms of physical and mental energy. There is no energy in any form to enable me to do anything. It is like dragging a granite stone everywhere you go. When I was at school, I had bucketloads of energy. Now, because of the sedation, I have none. The only way I can do jobs or tasks is to break them up into lots of little ones. I have to do this because I have more chance of getting them done that way. It breaks up the stress and energy that is needed to cope with doing anything. The more you ask of yourself, the more ill you feel. I have to gather so much mental composure in order to cope with the thoughts I am having when doing anything. Lack of motivation is the biggest issue of all for me.

From this discussion, it seems that the most productive way of moving forward in terms of motivation is to discover some coping and distracting strategies that might work for Cameron, so he is able to do more without the negative impact of debilitating thoughts. If he had some strategies to use while engaged in activities, then he may be able to undertake and complete them without too much distress.

At home, my best strategy for doing any jobs is to do one job, then have a cup of tea. Then do the second job and have another cup of tea. Doing things, a little at a time, is less daunting and much more realistic. It's possible to get a lot done using this technique without really upsetting myself too much. A word of caution is not to overdo things. If you are like me, I find the more I do, the more ill I become. You must find the right balance for yourself. I have some days where I simply cannot do anything because I am too ill. Don't feel bad if you, too, are in the same boat. Be reasonable in your approach.

Cameron needs recuperation time to recover from the psychotic thoughts that accompany the most mundane tasks of the day. From shaving, to making a cuppa, to brushing his teeth. Any task increases the intensity and number of psychotic thoughts, so they need to be spaced out or, preferably, not attempted. This also explains his need to know in advance what we will be doing so he can "prepare" himself, physically and mentally, for the challenges it presents.

Confidence

As a schizophrenic, I suffer "psychotic" thoughts continually – and I mean continually. These thoughts are usually violent, sexual, evil or perverse. These thoughts are the norm for me and occur spontaneously. You can't rely on these thoughts, so your self-confidence over the years becomes less and less, until you hit rock bottom. You have no confidence poker chips left. The degree of inappropriate thoughts makes me wonder, in a sense, if the wiring in my head is one hundred per cent correct. I feel that my brain cannot be trusted and relied upon, so where does that leave me? With even less confidence. We will term these four different "psychotic" thoughts as being "odd thoughts" as that label doesn't make me feel as bad. With a head full of these odd thoughts, what could make things worse? Things are made far worse by the fact you can't get rid of them. Something is very wrong in my brain, in this respect. In the past few years, while outside, I have only once successfully cleared my brain of a psychotic thought, as demanded by the situation. I was then dizzy for the next five minutes. Who would believe it?

Imagine child A has 100 confidence chips and is outgoing, and child B has 10 confidence chips and is timid. Both children are asked the same question. Child A gambles 5 of his chips on the outcome of the question and doesn't worry if his answer is correct, because he still has 95 confidence chips left. However, child B doesn't wish to gamble 5 chips, because that is half of everything he has. If he is wrong, then the damage will be almost irreversible. The confidence of child A is undiminished whether he is right or wrong with

the outcome, but it could be the start of the end of things as he knows it for
child B. Child B constantly gambles much more than child A. I suffer from
chronically low confidence levels – extremely and profoundly low levels. I do
not think I have met someone with as low levels as me, nor am I likely to. It
is shocking. I most readily match child B's situation, what with my paranoia,
seclusion and believing that my mind is being read.

I refuse to put myself up for scrutiny. I cannot run far enough away
from having to put my judgement or psyche on the line, because I know
my thinking is unreliable. People with confidence fare a lot better in life
compared to the unconfident. In fact, I believe that confidence is a massive
plus in your arsenal of tools to survive in life. The gulf between the
confident and unconfident is a bottomless abyss. I believe that confidence,
real confidence, almost brings another positive dimension to living. Whatever
way you look, confidence gives you an unmistakable advantage. Imagine
trying to be confident when you are possessed by a stream of psychotic
thoughts, as well as dealing with other people's conversations. I am lucky to
remain alive, never mind being confident.

T   Feeling confident and looking confident are two different
    things. In my line of work, I educate people to confront
    fears and inadequacies by learning how to appear
    confident when performing to others. Perhaps if you used
    some strategies to help you look more confident, you may
    achieve more positive results and therefore start to feel a
    little more confident on some level.

C   Yeah, maybe. It's not going to be a high level, even if it did
    improve a little.

T   Surely some improvement is better than a downward spiral
    of confidence?

C   Mm hm.

T   Do you consciously use any strategies to help you look
    more confident?

C   No, I can't say I do.

T   What characteristics would you say a confident person
    portrays physically? How do you know a person is
    confident when you look at them?

C	They are happy and smiling. Is body language a pointer? Maybe uninhibited body language?
T	What do you mean?
C	Waving your arms about… it depends on what you are doing?
T	I would say that a person with confidence is likely to stand tall with shoulders back, head erect and an open stance. They may smile and be happy, but that is more an indicator of friendliness, perhaps.
C	Yes, that sounds good to me.
T	Is that something you could start trying to do?
C	What? Standing tall and all that?
T	Yes.

We then practised standing tall with an elongated spine and shoulders down and back. Cameron's eyes remained closed and shut off, not literally, but they gave the appearance of being timid, so we practised raising the eyebrows to open the face a little more. We will see if it is possible to hold this kind of open and honest physical posture when we are out and about among other people.

Since the writing of this passage, we have discussed how often Cameron has been able to put this into practice. He said he has tried it once or twice. I have reminded him to do it on several occasions when we are outside in order to help him look less timid. Cameron seems distracted and unable to commit to this simple strategy, saying that he doesn't think about it when outside. This frustrates me tremendously as it is up to me to remind him about a simple thing. Cameron, in his defence, states that his instincts are to cope with his thoughts first and foremost. As a result, he has no brain space or mental energies to devote to the coping strategy of "walking tall", as all his energies are used in managing his thoughts. I suggested that he should think about using a positive strategy first and then use the remainder of his faculties to deal with the bad thoughts. However, upon reconsideration, we need to deal with our thoughts first – working from inside out. The only alternative is multitasking, attempting to do both things simultaneously.

I am sure that my confidence level is much lower than low – psychosis takes care of that. Being confident is a luxury I will never achieve. I can live with that now. It is not the end of the world, but I wish it wasn't the case. You can only do your best. Looking back, I can see I have been extremely unconfident. Since about the late 1980s, my enduring psychotic "anti-confidence" has remained unaffected. Unlike some other ailments, there is no cure. I am not alone with my problems. I remember seeing a man walking alongside a ten-foot wall, which formed the boundary of my local mental hospital. He was walking sidestep, facing the wall. My heart went out to him. I, too, can get myself in a real mess out there. I do know what it is like. Some people may ridicule him, but they do not know what psychotic thoughts he was experiencing at the time. If this man was anything like me, he would consider losing a limb to be free of psychotic thoughts. Because of psychosis, I am unable to make eye contact for fear of disturbing thoughts entering my mind and this is another big confidence destroyer. Not only do psychotic thoughts wreak havoc with your confidence levels, but they can put you in real danger if you don't know what is going on. Crossing the road, for example, is no easy task. The unconfident are the easiest of targets, globally speaking. Everyone dumps on the unconfident. As a result, they are treated very poorly. Being unable to change brings a tear to my eye sometimes.

I think that I frequently forget that Cameron suffers all day, every day. I am busy with my own thoughts and behaviours, planning and teaching; life takes over and routines get played out. I am not always consciously thinking about how my thoughts and actions affect Cameron. And yet he is probably spending all day with his thoughts thinking about how they are affecting me and him. I can be very selfish, as most humans are, in paying attention to me at the expense of others. I do not mean that I am deliberately unkind, but carers and those living with sufferers of mental illness do need to adapt in order to accommodate each other.

I am sure that I contribute to Cameron's feelings of low self-esteem and confidence. I tend to focus on physically getting us through the day in terms of actions and behaviours, and do not consider sufficiently his thinking processes and struggles with odd thoughts. Perhaps I do this myself as a way of self-preservation.

It makes me upset to think of the torment that Cameron endures each minute in his head. I don't think I could cope with what he does daily. It is a challenge for me to free-up enough of my thinking to carefully consider what I say and do and how it affects him. In our family environment, we like to be able to relax and to dispense with the niceties expected in the "outside" world. Family is where we can be ourselves, at ease with our inadequacies, and more tolerant of moods and comments as we let our guard down and chill out.

Cameron's confidence could be improved greatly if I were to consider more carefully what I say and do in the home. As Cameron spends most of his time at home, this is where he will learn confidence in himself first. It is unrealistic to expect him to be confident when outside if he is unable to be that way in the confines of home. My job involves the giving of myself, my energies, thoughts, strategies and creativity to others. That is the essence of teaching, the giving away of yourself to motivate and inspire learning in others. When I finish work, I can be drained because of "giving" all day and only want to "take" instead. Being considerate all the time when off duty can be hard work for me, but I think it is something that has the potential to really help Cameron build his confidence.

Anxiety and isolation

I don't know where to begin with this one. Anxiety is always with me, ever-present, varying only in intensity. When the intensity of anxiety is turned up, it is debilitating and commands a great deal of respect. If the anxiety (in my case) is intense enough for long enough, I lose the ability to speak coherently. And anxiety is one of the symptoms that you are supposed to be able to "deal with". How can you cope with paranoia if you can't cope with anxiety?

Anxiety permeates my life at the molecular level. It affects absolutely everything I do. This behaviour, which has been learned and reinforced over the years, must now be laid to rest and a more appropriate substitute picked from the vast range of possibilities still out there. I just hope I have the courage to affect these changes as required. So, instead of creating an atmosphere of anxiety or fear, why not try to generate an empathic, warm and positive aura. The possibilities are endless. Be yourself, choose your path and then go for it. I have a lot of work to do myself in this department, but the schizophrenic shackles are going to be tested to their limit as I try and fight anxiety.

Some of the things that make me anxious are loud noises, people talking and anyone walking toward me on the pavement, to name but a few. I feel possessed by the inability to control my thoughts. This is a full-on, strong experience. It is made even worse when it is a parent and child walking toward me and this makes me feel very threatened. It must have something to do with chronic schizophrenia isolation, or a strand of it. I have always been one for isolation. That Simon & Garfunkel song sums it up perfectly. Only do what you're comfortable with and look after number one.

T   Tell me what you mean by chronic schizophrenia isolation.

C   Isolation due to the illness.

T   Do you mean isolation from who you wish to be or isolation from other people, or what?

C   Isolation means that I shut all doors to other people. You ostracise yourself and stick your head in the sand.

T   So when you think you are in a negative position, or there is a possibility of you negatively affecting other people, you deliberately ostracise yourself?

C   No, it is just a blanket of avoidance of others in order to protect myself from feeling intensely uncomfortable. It is an automatic reaction not linked to conscious thought.

T   How do you consciously avoid others?

C   In advance. I would know the activity I am going to do and then plan and think through the activity. So, I plan what I am going to do and where I need to go, so that I can get the task done as quickly as possible.

T   Are there other strategies you use when out and about to avoid other people, apart from forward planning?

C   Yes, I walk really fast.

T   How does that help?

C   It reduces exposure.

T   I think it exposes you more, in that it draws attention
     to you.

C   It is supposed to reduce the time of intensity.

T   So less time in the anxious task is what you are
     aiming for?

C   Uh huh. Less time in the *extreme* trauma.

T   Have you spent any time looking at strategies to reduce
     anxiety levels, rather than reducing the time in the
     anxiety situation?

C   It is more a question of survival. There is no well-measured
     cure, no easy solution.

T   You are not answering the question: Have you spent any
     time trying to reduce anxiety levels?

C   Relaxing physically is a strategy I have tried.

T   Does it help?

C   Maybe a little, but not a great deal. It is trying to stay
     relaxed for a period of time that is challenging, rather than
     simply getting relaxed. A second is a long time when you
     are having psychotic thoughts.

T   Any other strategies you have tried?

C   Yeah, there is a thing whereby you can reduce the oxygen
     in your bloodstream by blowing out more than breathing
     in. It reduces the anxiety fire. It is difficult to remember this
     when you are outside. It can allow me to manipulate my
     mood and anxiety levels.

T   I am not aware of you using this when we are
     outside together.

C   I use it when in a waiting room or something like that.
     Making sure I don't fill up with air.

T   Don't you mean that your exhalation time is longer than
     your inhalation time?

C   Yes, that is what I mean. Breathe out over a count of six
     and breathe in over a count of four, for example.

T   There is a lot of free information about how controlling
     your breathing can help alleviate stress levels.

There is a very helpful article included in the Useful Webpages section at the end of this book that guides you through practising mindfulness and working on using awareness of breath to calm down in anxious situations by Diane Hamilton. After reading this, we discussed the usefulness of it.

T   Did you find this article useful or do you have any observations about its content?

C   It sounds like a good strategy to try and ease anxiety problems. It sounds plausible.

T   The breathing exercise was similar to what you said, but it stresses, as I would for singers, the importance of setting up a smooth repetitive pattern for breathing.

C   Breathing is very important because I do notice that I stop breathing when I am very stressed. I can stop breathing for about half a minute and I just forget how to breathe. I know it sounds stupid, but I just forget how to breathe.

T   What, for you, are the main symptoms of anxiety?

C   A really tense body.

T   Do you mean the muscles?

C   Yeah, you know, rigid and tense and block-like in movement. I breathe in but I don't really breathe out, if you know what I mean.

T   So you mean you hold your breath?

C   Yes. And I catastrophise: every little decision can be huge.

T   So you get rigid, hold your breath and are unable to make decisions?

C   Yeah. It is like being filled with terror. I need to get out of the habit of stopping breathing.

T   How are you going to do that?

C   I think people can hear me breathing and that puts me off as well.

T   Why does it matter if someone heard you breathing?

C   Because in my mind it would be them seeing or part-understanding what I am thinking.

T   This returns to the problem of mind-reading.

In the dictionary, one definition of isolation is, "lonely; cut off from society or contact". It's very sad that the illness can be so, so strong. I frequently isolate myself when I am in contact with others. I can fully understand isolationism. If you had the choice, would you choose to be in pain? I don't think so. A good few years ago, I read in a pamphlet that isolating oneself was an aggressive act. I interpret this as meaning that withdrawing yourself may be viewed as snubbing other people's needs. So how should someone who suffers from schizophrenia deal with this pain of constant bad thoughts when in contact with others? I'm not giving any advice, only a "bear in mind". I try and seclude myself by, for example, leaving the room, exiting the situation and ensuring that I do not become the focus of attention, so I avoid scrutiny by others. I sometimes talk to myself inside my head and use body language where I keep my arms tucked away or folded and have my head lowered. I will be trying to cope, but the "safety net" of isolation will always be there – thanks to the heavens.

T   Why do you think that tucking your hands away and lowering your head will not draw attention to yourself?

C   Because if you create eye contact, then that will draw more attention, won't it? For things to go wrong, you must engage the person somehow.

T   But you could stand with head up and arms hanging naturally at your sides and look down with your eyes if you wanted to avoid eye contact. I think it draws attention by tucking your arms away and lowering your head, because it is less natural. You could avoid eye contact without attracting attention by looking less natural?

I have deep-seated phobias about fire or flooding in the house. I see images of this happening that aren't there when checking that switches in the house are off and I can easily spend five to ten minutes checking this. If travelling somewhere in a car and it is doing over fifty miles an hour, I become inconsolable about feeling we are going to crash. I am so uptight physically that I feel like I'm going to explode. Recently, while being driven, I had ten panic attacks in ten seconds. They hit me, then dissipated, hit me, then dissipated. This happened ten times in quick succession. I

thought I should get a medal for that one! I live in the countryside and
understand people need to travel at the national speed limit. I am usually
traumatised by the time I reach town. I sometimes self-harm in a bid to
stay out of psychosis in the car.

T   Expand on the self-harm, please.

C   If you have something sharp in your hand and you keep
holding it more tightly, it cuts into your hand.

T   Does this help alleviate the anxiety felt when travelling
at speed?

C   Not really.

T   Perhaps it might be more beneficial to you, then, if self-
harming could be reduced while travelling in the car as it
does not seem to be an effective coping strategy – what do
you think?

C   Yeah.

T   Do you not trust the driver to get you to your
destination safely?

C   (Silence.)

T   So, what is it about driving at speed that is
the problem?

C   Just that something is going to go wrong, or there will be a
tyre blowout, or there will not be enough time to overtake.
The faster we are travelling, the worse I feel.

T   How many times have you been involved in a car crash?

C   Me? About three or four times.

T   Were any of these accidents with drivers who currently
take you places?

C   I am talking about when I was driving years ago.

T   So, we come back to the first question: do you not trust the
driver to get you to your destination safely? If you have not
yet had an accident, it is likely that they are safe drivers, is
it not?

C   Yes, but nothing is ever guaranteed, is it?

T   You can only be responsible for your own actions, not for
those of the other drivers on the road. Being a good driver

involves not only driving safely, but also dealing with any issues that are caused by other vehicles. We cannot predict the future and anticipate every fault of other drivers on the road, but we can drive in such a way as to be alert and ready to anticipate any issues and be ready to deal with them. Does that make you feel safer?

C   In a way.

When outside, a large percentage of my psychotic thoughts involve my feet and the nearest oncoming pedestrian's face. I quite commonly look like a fool as I try to fend off and shake away the psychotic images. I don't often succeed in this, but I feel great if I do, even if it is for a short-lived moment. If outside, I cannot, under any circumstances, establish eye contact, whether I am on foot or being driven, because all I do is have these largely disgusting thoughts that are usually violent and mutilative. How do you respond to someone about whom you have just had one of these terrifying thoughts? Eye contact sends me over the top. Eye contact, for me, is no longer an option.

T   How do you think things might be different if you were to walk tall with your eyes looking ahead or up, rather than down at your feet? Is this something that you have tried before?

C   I remember trying it one time, but I haven't really got a solution with that one.

T   Do you think it might change the nature of the psychotic thought if your eyes were looking elsewhere than the pavement and feet?

C   Not sure. I doubt it.

T   You have said several times that your psychotic thought comes as a combination of what you see in terms of feet, glass, oncoming pedestrians. So, if you were looking up at the sky, rooftops and shop windows, could this, theoretically, change your psychotic thoughts?

C   (Silence.)

T   (Persevering!) Have you tried this at all?

C   Semi-recently, I tried it by looking anywhere that might be safer to look, but I haven't really tried this much.

T   But if it is something that may make walking down the street easier, it might be worth pursuing?

C   Yeah, okay.

T   I mean, like a coping strategy. It might be worth trying?

C   Yes, oh aye.

T   It might help you to feel less anxious if we isolate situations that cause extreme fear and then talk through why they make you so scared. Are there certain conditions or situations that make your anxiety levels increase or decrease?

Cameron started to give lots of examples, so we decided that this was a bigger topic for discussion and we will come back to it later. He said that he does use coping strategies related to remembering a song or reciting a piece of poetry, using breath management skills and relaxation techniques.

Lack of concentration

Over the last year or so, I have noticed a definite deterioration in my ability to concentrate. I can go from forgetting about a single thing that has just recently been mentioned to forgetting a whole series of things. To be honest, I find it a bit scary when I forget the simplest and most obvious things. This problem is multiplied by my inability to check things quickly and accurately, such as the electric switches when leaving the house.

Alas, my overall concentration is diminishing, which I don't advertise readily. Tara suggested I take a memory check at the doctor's surgery, for which I got full marks – not sure how! An example of my lack of concentration could be when I am told day-to-day, simple things and then five seconds later I have to ask for them to be repeated. Tara tells me what is happening in the week ahead and I am unable to retain any of it, so I write it in my diary. The harder I try to concentrate, the more likely I will have a psychotic thought. You can only concentrate for as long as you have time without a psychotic thought.

T   What kinds of things do you do on a day-to-day basis that require some level of concentration? Are some things easier to concentrate on than others?

C   I don't know, but I am struggling to concentrate here and now.

T   Why?

C   Not sure.

T   What about watching and following a film?

C   Yeah, I have not really been able to follow the whole story or see the end of a film for a while.

T   I think that might be due to being sedated and suffering from disrupted sleep. You often struggle to focus simply because you are tired. What about your ability to concentrate on the telephone and hold a conversation?

C   I often forget where I am and get lost in it all.

T   Why might that be?

C   Just my illness.

T   I think your ability to concentrate is much improved when you are speaking to someone on the telephone compared with having a face-to-face conversation.

C   Yeah, I would agree with that.

T   Why might that be?

C   (Joking) It is all the practice I get in my sleep! (Cameron suffers from sleepwalking/talking.)

T   I think by "concentrate", you mean your ability to focus and think about the things that you want to, rather than being flooded with unwanted thoughts and images – is that correct?

C   Uh huh.

T   So, are you saying that your ability to control your thoughts has diminished lately, or are you saying that your ability to retain things has diminished lately?

C   Yes, I have a problem retaining things.

T   So why is forgetfulness an issue – or is it just a general worry? How is it impacting your life?

C   I think I am worried in general, but also notice that my inability to focus on things means I take longer to do things. This is because I have to check to make sure they are done many times, as I cannot trust my perceptions. I cannot focus and concentrate sufficiently to accept them as done and need to recheck lots of times.

T   This is part of your obsessive-compulsive disorder?

C   Yeah, I suppose so.

When I find myself in conversation, I always forget what I'm saying and have strong psychotic thoughts about myself. There is very little chance of being able to reciprocate a normal conversation.

T   Can you tell me more about the psychotic thoughts you have about yourself?

C   These thoughts are about how bad I am. Blasphemous against God. I think people can read my mind and then I have these sexual bad thoughts that I can't control, and they are blasphemous and totally offensive.

T   Can you tell me more about this?

C   Things that I hear, or words, or even completely mundane things all result in different psychotic thoughts. The louder the noise, the more harrowing the feeling. If someone coughs, I think they are having a dig at me. It's like, "Stop what you're doing. You're doing bad." If I am listening to the news and the newsreader is speaking about something terrible, then I feel really ill and start to feel guilty to the core. More serious things make me feel like I am pure evil.

I remember one time I looked out of the window to see a row of sunflowers near the neighbour's house. They were pointing in my direction. I felt as though the neighbours were having a go at me and insinuating that I am not

happy enough. I should be far happier. Bright and cheery sunflowers pointing
in my direction suggests that sun and brightness is needed in my direction – in
other words, I am not happy. Another example is when I was opening a packet
of painkillers. I felt sad by the way the previous tablets had been removed
from the packet. Instead of them coming out in horizontal pairs, they came
out vertically. I interpreted this as the male to female pairing being upset.
My brain acts as a factory, making weapons out of mundane things. It is so
intrusive and so upsetting.

Since writing the above, Cameron has been diagnosed with
sleep apnoea and has a continuous positive air pressure (CPAP)
machine and mask that he wears at night. It is a condition
whereby you stop breathing, especially when sleeping. I have
noticed a massive improvement in his alertness levels since using
this machine. He was also successful in stopping smoking and, as
a result, had his medication halved because his liver was "cleaner"
and absorbing more medication than needed. Before both of
these events occurred, it was very common for Cameron to sleep
throughout the day and in the car, and I really struggled to wake
him as his levels of sedation were huge. Happily, things are much
different now.

T   Do you notice a difference in your concentration levels
     since being on reduced medication and having the
     CPAP machine?
C   Yes. I can stay awake in cars now and when I am
     sitting in a chair. There is a slight improvement in my
     concentration levels.
T   How do you know there is an improvement?
C   I am awake all the time, so that is a good start. I can stay
     awake on longer car journeys – there was no way of doing
     that before.
T   What about watching films or holding conversations?
C   I think I can concentrate a bit better…erm…I can read
     things better and can concentrate a little bit harder. The
     focus is better.

Avoiding upsetting people

I have a terrible fear of upsetting or offending people. It permeates everything I do and think. It makes me look ridiculous at times. Taken to extremes, my behaviour can become psychotic. I think I upset people because they can read my odd thoughts and everything that is going through my mind. If someone can see and hear my thoughts, then they will think of me as a bad person because thoughts are private and not to be shared with others. My thoughts are disturbing and mutilative, and I feel very embarrassed and ashamed when I have these thoughts and people are near me. I usually end up trying to not make things worse. I don't mind how I get treated, but I have to really try and protect those around me. When things start to go wrong, I am usually desperate to save the situation, but at the same time completely helpless.

T   We discussed earlier that it is unlikely that people can read your mind. It is very unfortunate and sad that you are unable to believe that fact and realise that you are not upsetting people.

C   Okay.

T   Is there nothing at all that can help? Have you got strategies you try and use?

C   There isn't a magic wand to make things easier for me. You have to think yourself through it and it is very hard work. I am usually very edgy when I am dealing with people as I am trying not to upset them. I am shaking. The best I can hope for is indifference.

T   I don't think you upset people at all.

C   My mission is not to upset people, but I think they can read my mind. I find it mortifying.

T   I don't think you upset anybody, ever. In fact, you accommodate people all the time, are generous and very thoughtful.

C   But I still feel that I get mistreated at times. I can handle it, though.

T   Mistreated by whom?

C The public.

T How do you know that?

C You can tell because of how someone throws change into your hand, or the words they choose.

T I think you read far too much into what other people say and do.

C Yes, I agree with that.

T It is like you think that you are the centre of the universe and everyone's actions are a result of you and your mind.

C That goes back to the delusion of grandiosity, but you must try to not lose your sense of perspective.

The NHS website describes delusions as when a person has an unshakeable belief in something that is untrue. This may include believing that an individual or organisation is out to hurt or kill them. It may also include someone experiencing grandiose delusions where they believe they have power or authority over others. People who experience these thoughts are unaware that they are not really true, which can cause upset and distress.

I would agree that this is something that controls Cameron's behaviour very much. He can be very uncommunicative, even with me. By not saying anything, it is easier not to upset someone – a simple avoidance strategy. He often comes across to others as quiet and shy, but his reluctance to talk is very much driven by not wanting to offend anyone. Even with me and close family members, Cameron is unlikely to speak up if he disagrees with anything as he wants to maintain the status quo. He will not ask suitable questions of people for fear of saying the wrong thing or upsetting them by prying. His ability to make decisions well, even simple things such as what he would like to eat for tea, are affected. By avoiding conversation, sitting quietly, removing all attention away from him, Cameron is less likely to upset people as he isn't the focus of attention. The moment that others start to engage with him, "examine" him and have eye contact, the intensity and number of odd thoughts increases, along with the increased possibility of people reading his thoughts, over which he has no control. This would result in his upsetting people. It is very frustrating and sad that a belief in something like mind-reading can have such a debilitating effect.

CHAPTER 3
DAY-TO-DAY LIFE: CAMERON

I have unremitting psychosis/psychotic thoughts; there is no respite from these, which may include such things as broken glass or a sharp object in the face, toes of boots or the corner of something in the face. I am always having psychotic negative thoughts about myself – the type of thoughts you want the least. As hard as I try to concentrate, I cannot overcome the catastrophe of pedestrians or drivers being able to read my mind. I've tried everything.

T   What do you mean by negative thoughts about yourself?

C   It goes back to having thoughts about myself being evil and blasphemous.

T   Do you mean thinking of yourself in terms of behaviours that you would not want known to others and ideas that go against God?

C   Yes.

T   Do you picture yourself as acting upon these irreverent behaviours?

C   No. I am worried that people read my mind and think I may be like that. I am also worried that they can see all the previous wrongs and mistakes I've made in my life. The idea of this makes me feel worthless and ashamed.

Cameron has not been able to work in any capacity for more than twenty-five years and so he spends almost every waking moment at home doing normal, everyday things. His activities include maintaining personal hygiene, house chores, looking after the cats, an occasional round of golf, shopping, visiting family and so on. For those people unaffected by a mental health illness, these activities do not pose much of a challenge or a threat. For Cameron, however, each day and task has its own set of problems that somehow need to be negotiated.

Morning routine and OCD

Because Cameron takes so long to get out of the bedroom in the morning, I go downstairs and get the morning started: feed and de-litter the cats, make a pot of tea, go to the loo, tidy up and do any dishes sitting around, and feed the birds. By this time, if he is not already downstairs, I will go and bring him down.

When I wake up in the morning, I get dressed very slowly because I don't want to leave the room in case there is a disaster. I also worry that when I put on my deodorant that it might spray on the alarm clock and cause a fire. It doesn't feel like a remote possibility; it feels like it will definitely happen. I do try to rationalise things, but nine out of ten times, it doesn't work. Having been to the toilet, it takes about five to seven minutes to check everything is off. I can't concentrate and all I get is highly inappropriate visions and compounding emotions. For example, are the taps on or off? Will there be a flood? Is the towel too near the radiator and will it cause a fire? Even as I look at these things, I have already decided my brain is unreliable. All this does is diminish my frighteningly low confidence count, and it is majorly upsetting.

My anxiety compels me to check every electrical switch and tap whenever I leave a room. Every day, I lose a lot of time to OCD and psychosis. When I get up in the morning, it takes me about half an hour to leave the room. During this time, all I do is get dressed and check switches. And I leave the room in an agitated and very worried state because I can't be sure that I have switched everything off. Everything feels like life or death. I follow the same routine every morning. I continually recheck the empty electric sockets; I don't know why, but I do. During this time, I have an overwhelming sense of dread that I am going to do something dangerous. Then, I check two sockets that do have plugs in them. Between not being able to visualise it and my memory failing, I keep forgetting the thoughts I've just had and am not able to hold an image in my head because of violent and psychotic thoughts, which are extremely mutilative. I don't know what I am doing from one minute to the next and I experience desperately unwanted, intrusive thoughts. Every time I leave the bedroom in the morning, I think it is going to burn down.

T   What do you mean by mutilative thoughts?
C   Most of the thoughts I have are very bloody, like
        broken glass.
T   How can you see glass at a socket switch?
C   I don't have that image when I am checking switches.
        When I check a switch, I try to look at it and feel it and get

a reaction from my brain that it is off. When I look out of my eyes, it is as if my vision splits into four quadrants like a TV screen split into four sections. When I look at the bottom-left quadrant, I am more likely to have stronger odd thoughts, so I am limited with where I can look.

In my life, OCD involves repetitive checking. It has gradually increased in severity over the years. On a day-to-day basis, OCD is without compromise. Because I must constantly check and recheck things, my confidence, self-belief and happiness are readily replaced by fear, paranoia and upset. It fully disturbs my mind. So, daily, my feelings of wellbeing are truly destroyed – crushed like a tin can. OCD affects me by making me completely paranoid about turning off electrical switches in case I don't do it right. If I get water on the switch, then I go away worrying about an electrical fire, so I have to check my hands are dry and check the switch again. My mind is full of images of fire.

T   Can you see that the switch is not actually on fire?

C   When I am under pressure to recognise that I have done it correctly, my illness kicks in and I can't control the images that go through my mind.

T   Are you able to separate the image from reality? In other words, the "thought" from what is seen with the eyes.

C   There wouldn't be a problem if I could separate them.

T   The images that you see in your mind are what may happen in the future if the switch has not been correctly turned off, yes?

C   Mmm, yeah.

T   Do you check the switch with your finger?

C   Yes, and visually.

T   So, when you touch the switch, do you know which way is on and which is off?

C   Well, yes, I do know, but I can't feel much through my fingers. There is not much sensitivity. If I use my hand, I do know that it is in the right position sometimes.

T   My natural reaction here is to problem-solve because I am a teacher. I want to make them easier, more familiar, better controlled and so on. So, if your eyes are tricking you more than your sense of touch, perhaps you should rely on touch and less on the eyes?

C   Maybe.

T   You could change the priority of your senses from visual to tactile or auditory, so you would have other means to check, which may be more reliable and interfere less with your mind.

C   Even though I have checked a switch is off with my hand, it doesn't register with my brain that the switch is off. Nothing registers.

My OCD also affects my use of taps and the toilet. Using the bathroom is normal up to the point when I need to check things are switched off. If I haven't turned the tap off sufficiently, the sink will overflow and go on the floor and then make contact with electricity, thereby causing a fire. I repeatedly check the taps are off, but the image in my mind says they are on. I even check the toilet itself, but suffer psychotic thoughts and have images of flooding or electrical fires. I have mutilative thoughts about the window handle, the pointy bit that you hold on to open it with, and whomever I see or hear at the time. I have a routine to check things when I leave the bathroom: radiator, toilet, window, Xpelair and sink. When checking in order, I usually go back to the start if I have a psychotic thought. I've been ten or more minutes in the past just checking the bathroom. A psychotic thought absolutely smashes and splinters the window and I usually forget where I am, so I have to return to the start. I check the shower every time I use the bathroom, even if I have not touched the shower. I find the loop of checking and psychotic thoughts harrowing and degrading. Where does it all end?

T   We have overflow outlets in the sinks. We also have open plugs in the sinks and shower. This means that it would be impossible to flood any of our sinks or shower because the water would run away down the plughole.

C   I still wouldn't rule it out.

T   Even though the odds are in our favour, you would ignore them?

C	Uh huh. I understand you might think like that, but it is real to me.
T	It is a fear of something happening in the future, isn't it?
C	Yes.
T	How often have you been responsible for a fire or flood in our home?
C	Never.
T	Does that not give you any confidence?
C	Not really. Maybe it is because I have a deep-seated phobia.
T	Does it not make you feel better when I check the switches?
C	Yeah.
T	So, why do you need to check the switches if I do them?
C	In case you don't check them.
T	Do you not believe that I check them?
C	Yes.
T	Are you able, in any way, to understand the logic of the conversation I am trying to have with you? In other words, we have never had a flood or fire because of your inability to check things correctly and we have the backup of me always checking the switches, too. It is highly unlikely that you will cause these things to happen in the future.
C	Yes, I understand the logic. It doesn't help me to trust my judgement any better.
T	I am still confused as to why you don't trust me to switch things off? There isn't a problem about them being off, and no fire or flood. If I am the responsible person for switching things off, do you not trust my judgement?
C	My response has only one word: paranoia.
T	But I thought you just said in a previous sentence that you could understand the logic of it?
C	It is possible to understand a line of argument, but it is harder to understand the argument and believe it.

So, I am in the bathroom. I cannot use the bottom-left quadrant of my vision because of psychotic events that appear. I am having a stream of violent, psychotic thoughts all the time. When I am doing my list of checking, if anything breaks the chain of checking, then I have to go back to the start because I don't have a memory. I seem to have no short-term memory. I cannot hold an image in my head, because if I do hold an image and mentally settle on it, it goes psychotic immediately. I do not hold images in my head. I sometimes put my hands under the taps to check they are off and there is no water dripping from them. I usually draw a blank when receiving the information, both visually and by touch, so don't know if water is dripping or not. So, for example, if you were to cross the road, you would look one way and take in whether a car is coming, then look the other way and rely on your observations to keep you safe. But for me, if I do this, I cannot retain any images, as I always have psychotic thoughts that alter and confuse what I am seeing.

I am currently checking appliances a little too much for my liking. Different approaches for tackling the same problem yields different results. I used to lose a lot of heart when my attempts kept failing. It is like a combination lock – eventually something works. Never give up. You must be prepared to always try. Just keep chipping away. Let your psyche know that you're going to keep trying, year in, year out. Eventually, your psyche will accept this and change will become easier.

Having pets

For most of our married life, we have had a cat in the home. Growing up, Cameron always had a cat in his family home and I always had dogs and cats. We both love the companionship of animals. Cameron seems to get a lot of joy and happiness from speaking to, and looking after, our cats, Cloud and Honey. He, as do most animal lovers, chats away to them as if they understand everything he says. He has jokes with them, plays, talks, sings. He even plays music to them and strokes them in time to the music. His preference is for the smaller, older, female cat, Honey. I suspect this is because she is always getting beaten up by the bigger cat, Cloud. They were both housed with us ten days apart, but Honey was a rehoming and Cloud, a stray. They have never yet learned how to live together peaceably. I think Cameron likes to show solidarity with the downtrodden and so prefers to console, and be consoled by, Honey.

T   You like chatting away to Honey in the morning, don't you?

C   Yes. It is a pleasant distraction.

T   Do you worry that she can read your mind like humans, or do you know she can't and you can let your guard down a little?

C   Yes. I think that is a fair statement. It is being able to interact without pressure. I don't need to worry about being judged. When you are out, you are being judged all the time, but when you are at home with the cat, you can have some harmless fun.

T   So, she helps you to destress a bit?

C   Yes, definitely. It takes your mind off all your troubles.

T   Do you have psychotic thoughts about the cats?

C   No, I don't think I do, you know. I must just be so relaxed. Cats don't offend you with their actions and behaviours. They are friendly and reliable. The cats, like the birds, bring a lot of positive vibes to the house.

This is the first time I have heard Cameron say that he is able to undertake an activity without any invasion of psychotic thoughts. I am completely astounded and amazed and so pleased to hear this. I take it for granted that joy can be had from "simple pleasures", but I have never heard Cameron say this even once. You cannot underestimate the role of pets in family life as positive therapy for all members. Pets As Therapy is one of a number of UK charities that supply pet visits to those requesting it. In their mission statement, they state that they enhance the health and wellbeing of the community through visits by volunteers with their behaviourally assessed pets. They visit hospitals, hospices, nursing homes, special needs schools and other venues across the UK. They specifically state that working with animals can improve the lives of those suffering from debilitating mental health conditions by including assisted interventions as part of a holistic approach to treatment.

How often have you seen a rough sleeper or homeless person on the street with a dog? It is not surprising that those who are alone and isolated get so much from the companionship of having a pet. The Mental Health Foundation recognises the benefits that having a pet can bring to a person's life, giving purpose, playfulness, motivation and companionship. But perhaps for those suffering from intrusive and upsetting psychotic thoughts, they can offer true relief for a short period from their affliction. Each morning when Cameron blethers to Honey, I can now be comforted that, for that short while, he is in a better place and has some sense of relief from all the terror in his head.

Using the kitchen

In the kitchen, I never use knives if it can be avoided. Having been a psychotic fish filleter, knives just bring back an extremely unhappy world of very sickening thoughts. I don't need to be reminded of this world from my past as it was my most ill and unhappy time – the door to those memories needs to remain firmly closed. If you are having a really bad time and lots of invasive violent thoughts, the last thing you want is to have a knife in your hand. When dealing with knives, I have to sidestep a doorway to another world as best I can. I do not like exposing people to that sort of thing. It is so unnecessary and so upsetting.

T   Can you describe the kind of thoughts you get in a bit more detail or is it too traumatic?

C   I would be having a violent thought and I would then think, "How can this knife help me in this violent thought?"

T   Do you find it upsetting to talk about it?

C   I just find that having a knife embellishes the psychotic thought, makes it a stronger delusion, makes it more real.

T   Because you are holding a knife?

C   Yes. If you can have a violent psychotic thought about the edge of a clock, then you can imagine what kind of psychotic thought you might have when holding a knife.

T   I don't want to push too far, but to help the reader understand one of these kinds of disturbing episodes, can you give an example? What experience do you have if you are holding a knife?

C   I don't know because I don't really hold them. I never use a knife now.

T   Is that why you won't use a knife to cut your food up?

C   Uh huh.

T   Why have you never told me this before? (Unbelievable!)

C   I don't know. There is lots of shit I try to keep from you, you know.

T   But this book is to help people understand yours and my experience of living with this illness, so it is helpful to open up and share things. Why don't you tell me about these kinds of things?

C   I don't like dealing with these things myself, let alone pass them on. I have many doors that have been opened that are difficult to shut, you know.

T   Do you mean it is more painful to talk about them?

C   Yeah. It is a bit disturbing and really rocks your head.

I never use the cooker or make toast. I don't like switching on electrical appliances because I can't handle turning them off. The cooker is worse than the bathroom in that respect. I do, however, make cups of tea often, one of my greatest of comforts.

T   What is different about using the kettle to make cuppas?

C   Tea is one of my greatest pleasures. I find it lifts my spirits and cheers me up. I can't go out. What other pleasures do I have?

T   Does using the kettle traumatise you?

C   No more than everything else. I have thoughts about electrocution.

I do wash the dishes, even the knives, to reduce Tara's time spent on housework. She already does her fair share. In the kitchen, like everywhere else, there is no motivation to do anything. Tara does all the cooking to keep us both eating healthy food, for which I will always be grateful. Doing the dishes is about the only thing I do each day in the way of housework. In the last few years, my eating patterns have improved a lot. If you have no motivation to cook for yourself, or plan a meal, or be bothered with making any food preparations, your diet is likely to be poor. I do eat much more healthily now and have lost many stones due to a lifestyle change that Tara and I have both made. It is not surprising that you could just have a diet of ready meals and not look after yourself properly. Even putting a pie in the microwave to heat up can be hard work.

I have often wondered why many people with mental health issues can be overweight, but had not really given it much thought until now. In addition to there being issues with side effects from medication, if motivation is lacking, then the thought of planning and preparing something nutritious is not going to happen. The easiest of food to eat is likely to be what is in reach and quick. It has to be the least effortful of food. When lack of motivation is compounded with deluded psychotic thoughts about everything you encounter, then you want to avoid anything that upsets and sets off the psychotic violent thoughts. This would include plates and cutlery, as well as electrical appliances.

Using the telephone

I am really "phone-phobic". I will do anything except answer the telephone. If Cameron is in the same room, I will ask him to answer the phone. I am unsure why I dislike talking on the phone, but suspect it is because I cannot see the person's face that I am speaking to. This situation can be averted now, of course, with all the apps available for video calling, but even then, I would not opt to do this readily for personal use, though am happy to use it professionally. I notice that when Cameron uses the telephone, his conversation is less inhibited than when talking face to face with someone, especially if it is a social or personal call.

When using the phone, another aspect of my illness comes to light. As well as feeling that the listener can read my mind, I feel this is magnified by them hearing my breathing. The breathing noises are the arrows that "steer" people to reading my mind. So, after every exhale, that is the moment I feel I am being read like a book.

Another hurdle when using the phone is similar to walking away from the checkout operator: a very negative commentary kicks in, with very insulting language. When I start to end the engagement with the listener on the phone, I feel under a lot more stress than earlier in the call. I would like for the call to end well, with the listener thinking well of me. The moment of most stress is when ending the conversation as it triggers the profoundly insulting words in my head. At this juncture, I go to pieces and there is no way back from there. This insulting commentary is so intrusive that you feel really ill. Stress, in general, brings on the words in my head.

T   I think you handle yourself better on the phone than in face-to-face conversations.

C   Yes. I don't find it as intense on the phone as in person.

T   Why is it less intense?

C   Because you are not being physically watched. It doesn't matter how often you are blinking on the phone, as no one can see you. Everyone around you is not watching your every move, like it would be if you were in a shop or something. You are not being scrutinised so heavily.

T   Do you still have as many odd thoughts when using the telephone, or is it less than in a face-to-face conversation?

C   It is probably less, yeah. It is when it comes to ending the conversation that I get raised fear and paranoia because I want the call to end well. It affects the tone with which I am speaking.

Workmen

I find workmen quite difficult. As well as being able to read minds, they create all sorts of other problems. I find the noise quite upsetting. We had a door to the living room fitted a few years ago. The workman was hammering away, and the noise of the hammering was very detrimental on two different fronts. Firstly, I found the volume to be very threatening and secondly, the repetitive hammering noises seemed to feel like the hammering home of unwanted, intrusive thoughts, driving home the unpleasantries, like a violation of the mind, in a sense.

I usually put on music to try and cancel out any adverse effects, but because I am feeling so out of sorts, I usually end up feeling the music is talking about me. Then, I have to justify against what the music is saying about me. If this goes on for any length of time, I feel intensely ill. The longer it goes on, the worse I become. It gets to a point where I'm acting quite erratically, drawing attention to myself, and I distract the workman from his job as a result.

When we have workmen at the house, I will try and be at home and available to greet them. This takes the pressure off Cameron from the start as I can give a friendly welcome and give clear instructions and ask direct questions. It does not upset me having to engage with other people. If Cameron does have to deal with the situation, he will want to know how long the job will take, so he can gather strength for his inward fight with psychosis. It is always good to look after workers, so a cuppa and biscuit goes down well. Even this simple task can get Cameron agitated, as his psychotic thoughts increase and he has the "life-or-death" decision of which cake or biscuit, or mug to give them. These choices, for Cameron, can cause upset and he has to get it right. Everything causes anxiety and distress. Each "simple" decision has massive consequences and it is important that Cameron makes the right one so as not to offend anyone.

Smoking outside and being in the garden

I started smoking when I was nineteen years of age. I have always been a heavy smoker. I found smoking comforting. I was always a worrier and it just seemed to help. For many years, I found that I was unfit and my breathing was much worse than it should have been. Many people with mental illness are smokers, that's for sure. You are no longer allowed to smoke in the mental health hospital grounds. When I was first attending the hospital at Cornhill, everyone was smoking. There was a little smoking room, which was always packed.

I always wanted to give up smoking as I found it a burden. My health and money were the main reasons. At one point in my life, I thought I would be a smoker for my whole life – a very depressing thought. But I always had the thought that I would like to try to stop at the back of my mind.

I used to smoke forty cigarettes a day, if not more, because I was so anxious. I smoked for thirty years, but I haven't smoked for ten months with the help of an inhaler. By using the inhaler at the start, it seemed quite easy to stop. Then, I realised I was getting hooked on the inhaler. Still, I persevered. There was one morning when I could not find my only inhaler. We had to do a two-mile round trip to the nearest chemist as that was all I could think of – panic stations! Things went pretty well with stopping smoking. I had a few tougher days as the dosage on the inhaler was reduced, but it wasn't hopelessly difficult. Although addicted to the inhaler, the addiction was less than with cigarettes. As the dose was being diminished, I said to myself that I would, if needed, keep to the inhaler rather than cigarettes. I was fully confident that the inhaler was up to the task at hand. I still have the odd day here and there when I need a cigarette. I was surprised that, even after ten months of stopping, the urge for a cigarette could still be so strong.

I have now stopped smoking for several years since writing the above paragraph. I can enjoy different aspects of my life now. When you smoke, you only have your cigarettes and nothing else – it consumes your every thought. I can buy things that I couldn't afford before. I can engage in the spectrum of experiences that weren't available. You don't have to worry about where the next packet of cigs is coming from, so that is one less worry in the day. I feel healthier now and a lot richer! I don't really notice much difference in my mental health as a result. I am very pleased to have stopped. When you are a smoker, you are consumed by when you will get your next fix of nicotine. Once that addiction has been broken, you realise what a slave you were to it. The world suddenly opens up to you and the possibilities are endless. I am proud of myself for having beaten the habit.

I used to be a smoker for a number of years, but stopped more than ten years before Cameron did. It is a terrible addiction to have and very difficult to break. Not only do you have less cash and mess up your lungs and heart, but you also smell bad all the time!

I had resigned myself to Cameron being a smoker for the rest of his life. I used to nag him constantly to try to stop, but knew it was a waste of time. I refused to allow our new home to succumb to the smell and colour of nicotine. So, when we moved to our current home, I asked Cameron to smoke outside. What I did not realise until we embarked on this book proper was how difficult that experience was for him. There have been significant changes to Cameron's medications in the last two to three years as a result of stopping smoking. This has raised his alert levels and his susceptibility to psychotic thoughts. When we moved to this home, his doses were high. I comfort myself in this as I hope that he was more numbed than now to the detrimental effects of having to smoke in the garden.

I couldn't believe it when Cameron wanted to stop smoking. What I did know about him was that if he put his mind to something, then he would give it his all. I am so proud that he has been able to give up the crutch and burden of smoking. I think it shows him that he has lots of inner strength and fortitude. And he smells nice!

We have lived in our house for seven years now. It has a large garden and last year was the last straw with it. I was trying to help my wife by doing some hedge-clipping with manual shears. The following things were happening simultaneously:

1   A background stream of psychotic thoughts.
2   My mind being read like a book.

3 Having psychotic urges following psychotic thoughts. For
   example, when a neighbour is speaking, I would lunge forward
   in an urge with the shears to do harm to who was talking, like
   a paranoid, psychotic lunge. This lunge/thrust was happening
   every time I clipped at the hedge, so it was on a loop for every
   time that I opened and closed the shears as I tried to cut
   the hedge.
4 The loudness of passing traffic would strengthen the intensity of
   the psychotic thoughts.
5 I can't speak coherently as I am terrified, and this upsets me
   profoundly.
6 I feel like crying when I know I can't help my wife with work in the
   garden.
7 When walking on the garden path, I feel that the noise that the
   gravel makes advertises what I am thinking.
8 I can't breathe and I sound very out of breath.
9 I think people are talking about me.
10 Whatever I "let" my attention settle on, I have a psychotic
   thought about it.

I have always found being in the garden/outside stressful. In the last year or
so, with increasing pressure from my illness, I've lost the ability to "speak"
to my wife in a normal capacity. I now, of late, sound quite terrified.
This reinforces lots of bad thoughts in me and compounds the illness. The
problem is currently worsening. The root of the problem is that I feel as
though the neighbours can, through how my voice sounds, see what I am
thinking. I'm in a vice-like grip possessed by bad, intrusive thoughts and
I am terrified. Of late, I have had to console myself with the thought of
"no more gardens for me". It is an absolute non-starter. I cannot move for
psychosis and feel grossly ill.

   I am too scared to put the rubbish bin out on the roadside. I am way too
scared. If left all by myself, I would not do ninety per cent of what I do now.
People have difficulty understanding. I feel "too scared" to put out the bin. I have
a great deal of strife standing up for myself.

   I feel the traffic on the road is watching me and the drivers are plotting
against me, either for now or for the future. The higher the volume of the engine

revs, the more ill I feel, compounding my odd thoughts. It magnifies the already bad thoughts. My body is rigid through fear with trying to physically contort in a bid to control my thoughts. I'm trying so hard that I am practically convulsing. I am physically trying to force my way past psychosis, but it can't be done. I used to smoke and went in the garden to smoke. I stopped a few years ago, so now I don't have to go outside, which relieves me a great deal. Not going into the garden is not the end of the world. I should be grateful and count my blessings. I feel increased security indoors. This is probably why people with schizophrenia want to isolate themselves from society.

Travelling by car and shopping

How would you feel if you were supposed to leave the house for an appointment and you had to repeatedly check the same electrical switch for five minutes, having continual images of flames? Every single switch is a big, big problem. You've run out of time and are forced to leave the house with nothing but visions of fire. How would you feel if this happened to you? Upon leaving the house, paranoia consumes your brain. You must be sure with matters of fire. You must. My paranoia at every level makes me so frightened and it makes me feel that the end result will be wholly cataclysmic and catastrophic. This feeling of the end of the world coming permeates every level of thought. This sort of pressure can reduce a man to idiot status.

T   Are you worried for your life?

C   When in the house, I can be, yeah.

T   And when you leave the house, does it matter if there is a fire or flood if there is no one at home?

C   Of course it matters. That would be a major trauma event.

T   In what way?

C   All the animals would die, we would not have a home and might not be able to claim insurance.

T   These things happen to people and they get through it. Think of all the disasters we have seen on TV. I often say to you that when there is something to be worried about, I will tell you. Do you believe me?

C   Yeah, mainly.

T   So, if we lived in a house with no water and no electricity, would that help?

C   Well, it depends if there is a gas tank! (Laughs.) You need to be aware of dangers around you.

T   Being aware and taking precautions is all we can do, isn't it?

C   Yep.

T   So no point worrying about it beyond that. Worrying about every conceivable thing that could go wrong simply messes up with our current state of happiness and enjoyment of life. Once the dangers have been acknowledged and dealt with, we should move on.

C   We should, yeah.

T   Has it helped to have this conversation based on what you had written about OCD recently?

C   I think so, probably, yeah.

T   Can you say in what ways it might have helped?

C   Don't treat the same symptoms twice – in relation to having schizophrenia and suffering from OCD. It helps to get feedback from someone that isn't me. It has helped by comparing; I might think one way and you think another, but it opens up possibilities. The more you know, the better it is.

Being outside brings another dimension to the illness. I live miles from the city and only very rarely go there. I haven't been on a bus for about twenty years. If I have to go anywhere, I rely on someone giving me a lift in a car. The first problem with travelling in a car is doing more than forty miles an hour. I become increasingly frightened, but can contain myself – just. If the car I am in is overtaking, I tremble and start giving in to panic. People who live in the country usually travel at sixty miles an hour to get to their destination, as that is the speed limit. If we did forty miles an hour to stop me from being very upset, we would be beeped at by many, many drivers. There is no solution to this dilemma; we have to drive at sixty miles an hour. When overtaking at these speeds, I feel that death is imminent, and I am trying really, really hard to see if we can safely overtake. I can't juggle these manoeuvres very accurately. I am completely scrutinising every second of the manoeuvre and feel extremely unsafe. When the manoeuvre is complete, I breathe a massive sigh of relief, before getting ready to do it all again.

When travelling in a car, I feel so bad about myself. All I can think of is psychotic, mutilative thoughts. I feel I am failing in a manner that is simply just not on. So, if we take this feeling of self-evilness and multiply it by being mind-read, it is a wonder there is any sign of coherence in my life. If I do not try to contain myself physically, I would be flapping in an uncontrolled fashion like a flag. The only way I get through it is to make my legs and torso as tense and taut as possible. Whatever the situation requires, I try to maintain the rigidity without any relaxing. It is the holding on bit that is most difficult. I think I stop breathing somewhere during this palaver. When outside, this happens hundreds of times every trip. I think my body has forgotten how to breathe. This is most certainly caused by fear. The more the fear, the more I hold my breath so that I am practically convulsing.

Shopping is a nightmare. When I am in the shop and want to pick up something to buy, I am so frightened and consumed by fear that when I pick it up, I do so in a terrified and unconfident fashion. I pick the item off the shelf so gingerly that I leave myself wide open to humiliation, being belittled, and manipulation by others in the shop. I think they can read my mind. I sometimes snatch at the item to go in the basket or trolley. This usually comes across as over-aggressive or extreme. It is very easy to alienate yourself from everybody in the whole shop. You have to suffer humiliation like that, sometimes belittling yourself on purpose for the sake of the greater good. I think people can read my mind as I go round the shop or go to the checkout. I try with every molecule in my body to try and think of things that don't damn me or make me seem despicable, or do things that people can hold against me in the future.

So, there I am, going round the shop, bitterly frightened, totally insecure and with no confidence to help me. I feel I radiate perverse shockwaves – I try my hardest not to, but usually fail miserably. I think the wiring in my head is faulty and always takes me in a very inappropriate direction. After decades of this inappropriate channelling, is it any wonder I have no *confidence? I'm fighting for my life and I wish I could close with a happier ending, but I can't.*

People say it is good to be spontaneous; I agree with that. But with schizophrenia, spontaneity is the last thing on your mind. The prison population would rise exponentially if schizophrenics were naturally spontaneous. A spontaneous schizophrenic would act on urges. So, these perverse shockwaves usually radiate out every time I take something off the supermarket shelf. The main feeling I have is that this is harrowing, and it comes in surges, about thirty times on average for each shopping trip and each time I pick something off the shelf or place it back on the shelf. The resulting chronic depression is fully understandable because you can't do what you can't do. Shopping is usually the main trauma of my week.

I hate having to walk down the pavement on the side of a busy road. My inappropriate thoughts, more usually than not, take the form of a violent, psychotic thought involving my roadside foot and the driver of the nearest oncoming car. The image of my foot and the driver's face combine and you have a psychotic thought. This is very disturbing when you believe other people can read your mind. I would do anything to be in control of my mind and wipe the slate clean when needed.

Golfing

I have no motivation. My ability to enjoy myself is the same. There is no drive to get outside golfing. I go as a result of ongoing pressure. I am very worried out there. I joined the local golf club as a member, knowing full well I would not be able to mix in the clubhouse with all the other members. I feel very isolated in this respect.

T   What do you mean by going golfing as a result of "ongoing pressure"? Pressure from whom or what?

C   I take on board when you say that I should go out. And also the community psychiatric nurse (CPN) and support worker, who say that I need to get out of the house and break things up a bit.

T   But you enjoy playing a round now and again?

C   When the course is quiet, I enjoy the round, but not when it is busy. Busy is a nightmare.

When out on the course by myself, my head is brimming with negative psychotic ideas. I feel I have not made a good impression on the members. I've been a member for five years now and have never had a drink at the clubhouse. There are any number of social events taking place there: quiz nights, bingo, darts, pool and karaoke, and there is a restaurant. I am totally sure I will never be able to attend any such function.

One visit out of three, I have a support worker with me, so two thirds of the time I am on my own. My head is brimming with rude thoughts and I find myself swearing frequently and audibly at myself, but not too loud so others can hear. It is very seldom that I see another golfer when out for a round. I feel I am fighting for my life in a literal and social sense when out on the course. It takes three hours to go round, by which time I am brain-dead. On getting home, I usually need four or five hours of sitting and doing nothing to come back to any sense of reality.

It upsets me that all I have out there are odd thoughts. I feel so bad when I am trying to be nice. My thought process is like Russian roulette with a faulty loaded gun. I am always putting other people's broken tees in the bin and replacing divots and making repairs of the topsoil on behalf of others. I feel I look manic out there. I am tired of having odd thoughts. I could do with the occasional day off. In five years, I've only spent about ninety seconds in the clubhouse bar when I went to get a can of juice. The manager always says hello if he sees me going about the place and I feel included then. I can't relax on the golf course. I am usually rushing around manically, unable to reciprocate conversation with any passers-by. I am feeling very plotted against and my head is overflowing with bad thoughts.

I am looking for the odd moment when you hit a good shot and forget about all your worries for a moment. When I get home, I am very glad to be home. And although I may have played poorly, I am glad I got out there and felt a small sense of achievement.

I went for a game of golf on day 100 of the Covid-19 lockdown. I started the game very hot and bothered and hadn't had much sleep the night before. I was on my own, which I find very difficult. I played for about an hour, during which time I felt extremely tormented and that everyone was against me. I only played six holes and was continually shouting "Fore" unconfidently. It didn't seem to matter how I tried; every shot aimed itself at someone and I was very stressed. I accidentally rubbed my contact lens out of my eye, so had to stop playing. I was pouring with sweat and was feeling disturbed and immensely troubled. I walked back to base on a tarred road. Two pedestrians were walking toward me, about a minute away. I was already extremely uncomfortable. It was a long minute. I couldn't break the loop of the psychotic mutilative thought of my feet combining with the faces. This thought was repeating every few seconds. I didn't have the strength of mind to counter the thoughts; I was just enduring them. The pedestrians could see I was very weird-looking, uncomfortable, and very, very nervous. I somehow managed to say hello on the way past them. They didn't respond. I was picking up very bad vibes. I felt I was being seen as weak and that I was endorsing their dislike of me. This is a very common event for me. From a long way off, I was reinforcing their contempt of me and that I am worthless. I cannot stand up for myself and, as such, I am abused. Maybe this is because I have so many psychotic images and thoughts that I feel I don't have a leg to stand on. I don't know. But I can easily live with this abuse, which is a most basic experience for me. A couple of minutes further down the road, I was fighting off bad sexual thoughts about the next two pedestrians. This was compounded because I thought they could read my mind. I was trying desperately to extinguish some very trying thoughts. I was so distressed; I could not even tell you what the pedestrians looked like. It was not a good golfing day.

CHAPTER 4
DAY-TO-DAY LIFE: TARA

I have always been active in music. I started piano lessons at the age of eight or nine, and violin lessons a year or so later. I cannot imagine my life without it. I have many interests, but music is my blood and soul. Over the years, I have learned to play other instruments and to sing, undertaken examinations, performed in festivals and concerts – the typical path for a young musician. There was only ever one road for me as a career, so here I am.

After gaining a first class honours in teaching music (BEd Mus) from Aberdeen's College of Education in the 1990s, where I met Cameron, I taught for a short period in secondary schools and then succeeded in gaining full-time employment at Aberdeen's College of Further Education. There, I was lucky enough to work with music teaching diploma students preparing for careers in instrumental and singing teaching. While studying and working, I also gained teaching and performing qualifications in singing and piano from various UK conservatoires. So, while teaching classes of music students, I also worked with individuals teaching piano and singing technique and performance.

I very much enjoyed my full-time teaching career, but always wanted to be able to set up my own teaching studio practice, teaching others to sing and play. Singing became my passion over the years, as I came to it later in life and found it all absorbing. Each person's voice is unique to them and each student voice comes with their own unique needs, habits and aspirations. I became increasingly passionate about healthy vocal function and how to get the most from one's voice. Coupled with the ability to create music, learn poetry and languages, use drama, characterisation and storytelling skills, as well as manipulating and controlling the voice, it spurred me on to study for a Masters and Doctorate in my singing teaching practice.

I have always wanted to work for myself and to set up a studio, choosing what to teach and to whom. It would mean having more control over the educational decisions and working cooperatively with individuals and groups, helping to achieve success and progress, and developing potential. After I discovered the wonderful world of singing, I became more passionate in realising this aim.

However, as the sole earner in the household, with a mortgage, it was not an easy decision to make. I could not afford to leave my full-time employment until I had built up a sufficient client base for private teaching. So, this meant there was a period of time when I was working seven days a week as I tried to build up the number of private students I had. There came a point when I had to take the plunge and leave my full-time work and devote my energies to building up my private teaching practice. While it was not easy financially in the first year or so, I am now well established in my private teaching practice and work from my studio at home.

There are other reasons for endeavouring to work from home rather than in an educational establishment, as it means that I am around and available for Cameron each day. I think my presence at home helps him feel less frightened, more safe and secure, and as I do not have much travel time added to my working day, I am able to spend more time with him. Being self-employed also means I have more flexibility about when I work, so I am available, most times, to help with taking him to appointments, collecting medication and so on.

Most students I work with are both singers and adults. Through being the music director of Banchory Singers community choir, I come into contact with many singers who wish to improve their abilities with a view to getting more out of their time in the choir, and achieve greater success and satisfaction from the endeavour. Working with adults is a joy. Just as many children attempt to learn an instrument, there is no reason why adults should not be afforded the same opportunity. Many make tremendous progress. One does not need to learn to sing or play an instrument to become a performer or make a career from music. Learning to play or sing is a highly rewarding and challenging activity, and I feel very privileged to be a part of the process. Most people I encounter assume that I mostly work with children. In a similar way to adults, the majority of children will not follow a music career path, but they can still learn the discipline of progress and practising, the social skills needed in cooperating with others, sharing in music performance and the therapeutic benefits of making music.

In our busy world of work and family and/or our quiet, solitary world of retirement, music can be both a distraction and a focus, a way of passing time constructively and an outlet for expression. I have come across adults in many different situations socially, financially and culturally, but have discovered that all can find learning to sing or play stimulating and satisfying. It allows for greater appreciation of the thousands of musicians that we hear around us, and provides an insight into the hours of practice required in order to become competent in performing.

I work from my studio in Alford two or three days a week and used to travel to Banchory to work from a church hall one day a week. The church hall allowed me to work with several people who did not drive, as the hall was on a bus route and allowed for prospective students to choose a location for lessons that was closer to their home. The disadvantage, however, was that I did not have access to my full range of teaching equipment, including notated music, which forms a fundamental part of learning to sing or play. I have been moving toward working less days but longer hours, so that Cameron and I have more days together. Cameron used to suffer from the effects of sedation from medication, so he often stayed in bed, sleeping most of the morning. It made sense that I worked when he was resting, then on the days when I was not working, he was sufficiently rested for us to enjoy time with each other. This routine has now changed and I work solely from home.

Cameron is not required to interact with students that I teach as the music studio is in a separate building from our home. This helps to alleviate anxiety and other symptoms for Cameron. He is, though, very helpful in taking messages by telephone, which is great for me, and I can follow these up at a later time. Much of my work away from students involves keeping on top of appointments, rearranging times when needed, emailing newsletters and information concerning concerts, exams and festivals, and keeping students informed of anything else related to music learning and performing. In addition, there may be recordings to be made and emailed out, music to be transposed into more suitable keys for singers, lyrics to be scanned and emailed, and so on. Administration takes many hours each week. Banchory Singers community choir rehearse for just over two hours each week in the evening, so this also requires me being away from home. I also examine for London College of Music, which requires me to be away from home a few days at a time. I perhaps only have one trip away as I know Cameron finds it difficult being at home alone.

Twice a year, I arrange for students to perform to each other in informal concerts that are open to the public, but it is mostly friends and family who attend. These are usually in an afternoon so as not to clash with evening commitments and means that families are more able to join in. I have set up a series of free events in collaboration with Newton Dee in Aberdeen, which take place eight months of the year on the second Saturday of the month. These are always at 5pm for less than an hour in the wonderful setting of the Phoenix centre. It allows a performing opportunity for music students, but also for professional and amateur musicians in the area to perform and share their music. We also sometimes cooperate with practitioners from other art forms, such as dance, drama and poetry.

Banchory Singers community choir arrange and perform at four concerts each year – two in the spring and two in December. In addition, they are often asked to sing for charity or community events, especially over the festive period, and they sing at festivals and competitions. They have also hosted choirs from abroad, as well as travelling to Europe to perform. They have workshops and social evenings and are a busy choir.

I perform within the duo "The Great Dames" with Ceri Kindley and regularly have performing commitments within the local community at church events, festivals and concerts. This involves finding time to rehearse on top of an already busy weekly schedule and sourcing new and appropriate material for each concert. It is great fun as we do a wide range of repertoire from traditional to operatic and we both enjoy our humorous songs that get everyone laughing. We even released a CD called "Venit".

I have always been involved in playing the piano for people as an accompanist. I love playing the piano, but have never been good enough or disciplined enough to be a soloist, so accompanying has been wonderfully useful as well as enjoyable. When I worked at college with instrumental and singing teaching diploma candidates, I played for most of the orchestral instruments and singers that required accompaniment in their practical examinations. All of my singing students require an accompaniment, and while backing tracks are available, it is always musically safer to have a live pianist who can cover up any errors made and can slow down and speed up as the performer wishes. I am asked to play at concerts when an accompanist is needed for instrumentalists or singers. Sometimes these concerts require a bit of travel and so I tend to weigh up whether I can fit it in around all the other commitments I have. I am also asked to conduct at workshops and "come and sing" days, or to perform as a singer soloist. So, there are always performing or music-making events interwoven into my weekly teaching load.

Many of these concerts and events will not impact much on Cameron, as they involve me being away from home. He will simply not have me at home for the duration of the event and will not have the added stress of being in a position where he is forced to interact with others. This, however, is not always the case. Cameron does like to come and support me in what I do and usually comes to the free monthly events, the student informal concerts and Banchory Singers concerts. Having to mix with people is very trying for him, so after attending a music event Cameron is usually exhausted and likes to have quiet time to mentally recover. He will also usually need extra rest the following day. As I have been a performer and teacher in the local area for a significant number of years, I am quite well known and as Cameron sometimes attends, too, he is also well known. Often, he will say that someone spoke to him, but he did not know who it was. Because he has to protect himself and others from psychotic thoughts, he tends to avoid eye contact completely, so when we are in company he will often not take in any details of people or situations, other than those that may affect him mentally and emotionally. As a result, he tends not to know what people look like, even though he may know names from conversations we have had. He would be no good in an identity parade!

In addition to not really connecting and communicating with people at these concerts, he doesn't really seem to connect with the music either. When I ask Cameron if he has enjoyed the event we have attended, what item he liked best, what he thought of my outfit, or which song he thought was best performed, he is unable to give any answers, more often than not. Although his body is in attendance, his mind is elsewhere when there are people around him. This is due to the uncontrollable thoughts that permeate his mind and his mental attempts to hold things together – not giving away his thoughts to others, for example, and other strategies to help him cope with every moment.

At home, in a relaxed environment, Cameron is an avid music listener and gets much enjoyment and therapeutic release from listening to music. It is a shame that this cannot be carried through to the joy of live music. As a musician, I am frequently encouraging musicians and learners of music to embrace live music as it is a totally different experience to listening to and watching a recorded performance. Before the invention of sound recording, all performances were live. There is an added vibe to live performance, as it is music made in the moment and anything can go wrong at any time. The element of risk-taking adds an edge to the performance. Equally, there is a spontaneity and magic that can happen as we focus and connect in each second and are consumed by the task at hand. I am not saying that recorded performances cannot also be magical, but there is something so very human about the shared experience of live performing and acoustics. Sound vibrations may be physically felt throughout the body rather than only appreciated through aural perception. It can be a sensory and emotional experience.

Because I work with many practising musicians and artists, I am often asked to attend events in which they are participating. In addition, there are often concerts taking place that I may wish to attend as an audience member. Because I know that it is too trying for Cameron to attend public events, I tend not to go to any extra events other than those that I am organising or participating in. I am quite frequently asked to attend events by people I work with or know, and when I say I will not be going I think they wonder why I am not supporting local artists, local causes and the community. Because people do not know the details of my personal life, they perhaps think that I am uninterested or lazy or simply snubbing them. I do not hide the fact that Cameron suffers from schizophrenia. In fact, I find it helpful if people do know, as it helps to explain some choices that I make that may appear strange to others.

Very occasionally, say once a year, Cameron and I will attend an event together – something that I, or we, would really like to see at the cinema or theatre, for example. I suppose you could argue that I could attend events alone (which I do occasionally), without my husband, but the decision to do that means that I highlight the fact that Cameron is not with me, which probably makes Cameron feel worse for not being able to support me – and who, in all honesty, wants to go to an event on their own anyway? As I said before, it is much nicer to have a shared experience, where you can discuss what was seen and heard with someone who was there. And I suppose the main reason that I do not go alone is because I do not want Cameron to feel inadequate by not going, or to feel bullied into attending. Marriage is about caring for and loving each other through the difficult things. So, while I do miss not going to more music and theatre performances, I would rather have a stable and secure relationship with my life partner.

With my wife's career firmly entrenched in music, I find myself in an extremely uncomfortable position in that I have to go to concerts regularly. I lack confidence on an acute level. Most of the time, I survive by sitting in the back row and way off to one side. I have no confidence to sit at the front and have my body language scrutinised. Sitting at the back also helps, to my mind, by not allowing performers to see my face when I'm having psychotic thoughts. The last thing I need is for them to be in any way affected by my illness. With all this going on, one doesn't enjoy all the concert, but at least you see some of the spectacle, for which I am grateful. Make no mistake, it is extremely hard work to sit through a concert and keep it together. I use the same philosophy when going to the cinema. I sit in the back row and way off to the side. This means there is no one to scrutinise you or your behaviour. It is easier at the cinema than at a concert because I am not worried about upsetting the performers.

I am happy for Cameron to sit to one side when we go to an event together, although I would prefer a better view and sometimes we negotiate to move a little more forward and less to the side, if possible – especially if the event is dependent upon the ability to see action. It is not so important where we sit at a music concert, but at the cinema or theatre it is nice to have a good view of the action, especially with the rising cost of tickets.

CHAPTER 5
MEDICAL SUPPORT AND MEDICATION

The website "Living with Schizophrenia" is a useful resource and gives a good description of modern treatments for schizophrenia. Because the brain is such a complex organ, it follows that treatment for its disorders will be equally complex. For schizophrenia, it may require a drug combination to successfully alleviate psychotic symptoms rather than on a "fix it all" medication. It also states that different people respond differently to different medications. A psychiatrist is usually the person in charge of medical prescription and monitoring the effectiveness of the treatment, but it may take some period of time to establish the optimal levels of medications. The medications used to treat schizophrenia are usually termed antipsychotics or neuroleptics and they frequently have a sedating effect. They are not used specifically for this reason but because they effectively help to relieve the psychotic symptoms.

The not knowing I was really ill for two years or so is a body blow that I am still fighting today, surreal as it sounds. I have once been lost in the psychotic ocean; ill at work in the fish house in the late 1980s with florid schizophrenia for one to two years before I was diagnosed. I became more ill as time went on. I had no family support, no caring boss, living alone in a caravan with no real friends, no medication and no psychiatrist. At work, everyone knew I was ill except me and nothing was being done about it. The longer you are in the sea of psychosis, the more things change. For example, something simple like table manners can be forgotten. Not to worry, though, as these smaller problems can be dealt with after the bigger problem of successfully breaking the psychotic hold that the illness has over you. Life was sheer hell. Living alone in a caravan with no partner, no heating, snowdrifts outside a lot of the time and food in short supply. Life was a titanic struggle and I soldiered on blindly. I decided one day to get a sick note for a week and hand in my notice at the same time. The doctor who saw me said I needed help. I was referred for mental health treatment. My nightmare world was to be replaced. Tablets lessened my symptoms and my whole way of life changed overnight.

When I was at school, I used to draw strength from the fact that I didn't have mental health problems. Quite the reverse. I represented my secondary school in five different sports, was class representative and member of the class quiz team. In my last year at school, I was in a staff versus student quiz, and another time I was asked about a TV quiz. After a diagnosis of schizophrenia, I am too frightened to even bring in the wheelie bin from the roadside.

My first encounter with mental health services was around 1988 or 1989. Nobody told me I had schizophrenia. I agreed to a short stay in the Royal Cornhill Hospital in Aberdeen so as to keep everyone happy. One evening, in the smoking room in my ward, a guy asked me what I was in for. I didn't have an answer and felt like a bit of a fool for not knowing what was wrong with me. It was then that I realised I had to talk with my psychiatrist.

T   How many people were in a ward?

C   On average about twenty people.

T   Were the wards mixed gender?

C   Not in my ward.

T   How was the decision made that you had to go into hospital?

C   I left my filleting job and the doctor said I needed to get help. So, an appointment was made at the local mental health clinic and the psychiatrist I saw suggested that I voluntarily go to the hospital to see how ill I was and to be monitored. I initially refused to go to the hospital, but I was continually asked to do so, and eventually gave in.

Life in the hospital was pretty grim. The staff were excellent, but even excellent staff can't stop you from dying of boredom. Boredom is my main memory from my time spent there. Each ward would have a half-hour aerobic-style class. A movement or dance teacher came round the wards with a portable stereo system and you did relaxation and movement. I didn't enjoy these sessions at all. They made me cringe. I attended two groups over the course of the week. Lunch group was where you learned to plan a meal, write a shopping list, go to the shops for the supplies and then return to the hospital to make the meal. The other group I went to was to play nine holes of golf. I don't know what happened to all the other hours of my waking day. The man who ran the golf group was genuinely the most positive man I have ever met. He was truly positive and happy. This positivity was unrehearsed; he was spontaneous and effortless in his way and manner. While in the hospital, I would walk to visit my mum every day. It would take an hour to get to the house and an hour to walk home. It helped to alleviate the boredom and to pass the time.

After five weeks at the hospital, I decided to leave so that my giro (money) wasn't docked. Because I hadn't had to be sectioned, I was allowed to do this. While in the hospital, I struck up a nice friendship with an older man called Jim. We met at the lunch group and I found him to be a very polite and friendly man. One of a dying breed of gentlemen. I won't forget Jim. That five-week stint was my only residential stay at the hospital. I heard recently that with all the budget cuts the team leading the groups is run by just one person; it used to have four or five members of staff organising and implementing activities for all the wards back then.

Since 1988, I have been on perhaps ten different medications, all of them at a regular dose. For the last twenty years, I have been on a medication called clozapine. It's not straightforward trying to find the best dosage; it can take time to perfect. Everyone is unique and responds differently to tablets. This is surely no easy task for the psychiatrist to decide. Adjustments are the norm as your life unfolds, adapting and improving the tablet dosage as you go on.

Great, thought I. Looking forward to my next medications. Straight away, a problem emerged. I became so dizzy. I simply couldn't stand up straight and my knees buckled. I felt as if someone had dropped a huge weight on my shoulders. All this led to the result that I wasn't safe to stand. Do not assume this would happen to you. We are all very unique.

It is better to repeat yourself ill than to assume the psychiatrist knows and be more ill. I can't believe I was left so depressed for so long. I thought the psychiatrist would easily recognise that I was heavily depressed. I assumed, but I was wrong. I experienced being unhappy much, much longer than I should have. I have tablets to help tackle depression now. Nobody wants to be sad, so make sure you tell your medical specialist because they cannot read your mind. I remember my mum saying to me a few years ago, "God doesn't want you to be so sad." She must be right and I wish I had asked for help a lot sooner.

I think psychiatry has progressed a long way in the last thirty years. I was very impressed by my psychiatrist's ability to choose the right tablets and the right dosage. This bodes well for the younger generation with problems like my own. Newer tablets are much less sedating and more finely tuned to do the job they

*are meant to do. A lot of the older tablets just give a blanket of dulling effects,
which leave you less bright, less alert and a bit hazy round the edges. The future
looks good in the advancements in both psychiatry and medicine. Maybe the
future advancements in medication will mean that we won't have to fight quite so
hard for positivity. But it is better to fight for the positive rather than not try. At
least you're trying. Looking ahead long-term, tablets will improve, meaning the
intensity of suffering will diminish. So, let it be.*

Side-effects of medication

Wikipedia states that the medication clozapine, sold under the
brand name Clozaril, is an atypical antipsychotic medication
and is mainly used for the treatment of schizophrenia, especially
in cases where psychotic symptoms did not improve following
trials with other medications. It may decrease the rate of suicidal
behaviour and is more effective than other typical antipsychotics.
It is usually administered orally or by injection. The website
continues to say that clozapine is associated with a relatively high
risk of low white blood cells, a condition linked to immunity, and
so those taking this medication need to get regular blood tests in
order to monitor the white blood cell count. Other side effects
include seizures, heart inflammation, constipation, high blood
sugar levels, drowsiness, increased saliva production, blurred
vision and dizziness.

*Clozapine medication is your last-chance medication. Usually, it is only given
to people who are resistant to the slightly older antipsychotics. I think this
"wonder drug" is a bit overrated. There are many side effects – the same as
all medication – but the main one is that I feel extremely drowsy most of the
time. Clozapine may lead the way, but, in my opinion, there is a long way to
go before the perfect meds are found. You have to have regular blood tests to
monitor the white blood cell count. I have blood tests every four weeks. The
white blood cells are responsible for fighting infections, such as a sore throat. If
you don't have your blood tests, then you get no tablets – that was made very
clear at the start.*

I have found, over the years, that all the medications for schizophrenia have led to slight weight gain. This "heavier" person is then aggravated by low confidence and low self-esteem – dangerously low. Clozapine is no magic wand. For me, another side effect is unquenchable thirst. I drink tea, coffee and diluting juice all day long. I also get severe constipation as a side effect and have to take two different laxatives. I'll be on medication for the rest of my life. That doesn't worry me. Going back in time, I was twice given a test run of no medication and both trials resulted in a really fast deterioration into the bottomless chasm of psychosis. After the second trial, I realised I had to take tablets for the rest of my life. I am grateful for all the help, medication and support I've received over the years. I'm also very glad that I can see that I am ill. Knowing you are ill is the first step of one epic battle.

Just over three years ago, my doze of clozapine tablets had to be reduced. I was so sedated for so long before this time and I had developed sleep apnoea. I couldn't stay awake on car journeys; I was sleepwalking and moving furniture in my sleep; I was getting into the shower fully dressed at three in the morning. I used to sleepwalk and fall asleep standing up in the bedroom and then have a crashing fall. One time, I fell against a door and dislocated my finger and we had to get straight in the car and go to A&E. If I got myself comfortable in a chair, I would be asleep in no time at all. Sometimes, during the day, I would still be sleepwalking. For example, my wife would be knocking on the door to get in the house. I would get up from sleeping in the chair, go to the door on hearing the noises, speak to my wife, then not let her in.

The sleep apnoea machine (CPAP), which pumps air into my lungs when I am in bed and asleep, has been a revelation. My crashing falls while asleep soon stopped. The machine also takes note of how many times an hour I stop breathing and calls it "events per hour". Last time I looked, it was some ridiculously high number. I discovered only recently that this stopping breathing can cause trauma to your pulmonary system. I now make a conscious effort to reduce my inadequate breathing due to stress and try to breathe out more, even though it feels difficult. If you are stopping breathing once every five minutes when asleep, that is a great deal of trauma you're putting your heart through. So, when you are awake, you must make the effort to reduce the overall stress to your system.

As I said, I had my dose of clozapine reduced a few years ago. The biggest downside to having my medication halved is that I have more severe symptoms, *like feeling that my mind can be read and thinking psychotic violent thoughts. The end result is that you feel unwell and are in a lot of pain. You have to try and find a way of living with the pain. I find taking things one day at a time helps. Since being on a reduced dose of clozapine, I have made the conscious decision to try and be a lot happier with my lot in life. Things have never been easy. I know things are awful out there, but when I am at home, I try to be happy about being at home. Ninety-five per cent of my waking day is spent at home, so let's be happy because we are home.*

Since my medication was reduced by half, I feel that I have emerged from a bit of a dream. Parts of me are more ill (increased number and intensity of odd thoughts), but in other ways things are better. These days, I can read better. I try to rationalise my way out of many daily events and I think maybe I can focus a little better on specifics. In my opinion, medication knocks the stuffing right out of you. You have NO enthusiasm, NO drive, NO excessive joy, NO motivation – but at least you are alive. Hopefully you can enjoy music in some form and you can enjoy the different colours in the garden. You can look at the wildlife and be entertained. I will be happier now. I realise most of my time is at home and maybe there will be improvements all around because of this.

I haven't been on such a low dosage of clozapine for many, many years. I feel a little more awake, a little sharper, a little more involved. I do see some cracks in the wall, such as increased issues with OCD. I can live with this, but need to keep a close eye on the intensity of it. I am a little more involved in conversations, albeit on a very basic level, but it pleases me that things are moving in the right direction. I don't have many friends, but one friend did tell me once that the intensity of the illness diminishes as you get older. I see the wisdom of that and can draw some strength from this.

Life is still very demanding, but it pleases me that I am able to do more. It still causes stress, but not as much stress as it used to. I can do more now before I reach my stress limit. The more I do, the more I get stressed. If I take on too much, I become very upset, almost disturbed. I can't think, can't concentrate, can't take anything in, can't function. The toll is severe. With this illness, you have to deal with terror, continually controlling voices, delusions, mutilative visions, people reading your mind, manipulated emotions and on and on. When we can't take any more, we've had an extremely trying and disturbing day. This should be recognised and respected.

After twenty-five years of compulsive checking of switches and taps, I decided to ask my psychiatrist if there was any medication for OCD. To my absolute horror, there appeared to be. So, for twenty-five years, I had been carrying this deadweight, this big soul-destroying mess, resulting in endless upset. Do not wait twenty-five years to ask about any form of medication. You must look after yourself first. I made the mistake of believing that people could read my mind, so I thought it was known that I needed help with OCD. Don't assume they know. I won't take things for granted again where medication is concerned.

Community support

I have a support worker and a CPN. I see the CPN every few weeks in my home. I usually see the support worker every two weeks and if it is golfing season, we will go to the course together. With the CPN, I discuss medication, anxiety, current difficulties, coping strategies, meditational websites and the like. These people are very sensible in what they say and they do a good job. Over the years, I have always been quite impressed by the services offered. These workers exist for people who, like me, have no friends in the traditional sense. They help to stop severe isolation and act as a social safety net where applicable. If it were not for these services, people would disappear from the map altogether.

When Cameron has a visit from a CPN, I will usually leave them to talk alone. I think it is important that he has space to talk about his concerns openly without worrying about saying things he doesn't want me to hear or know about. It helps to have a specialist to guide him and make suggestions for strategies he might want to try to alleviate his anxiety. It affords him the chance to chat about his week and what he has found stressful. It also means that he has to talk for himself, as I am not in the room to do it for him. I would not like these professionals to think that I put words in his mouth.

I have had some negative experiences with CPNs and this is another reason I tend to stay away when he has a visit from one.

I have very strong opinions about medication and had raised this point at one appointment many years ago. My words were taken the wrong way, though. I was referring to *me* taking medication. If I think there is another way to treat things, I will try that first and only resort to medication if nothing else can be done. I was talking about me, not Cameron. Equally, though, I would not want Cameron to be forced into taking more medication than is necessary. A note about this was taken in his file and it has affected how CPNs view me. When we have a new CPN to visit, they read his file and find out about the unsupportive wife who is anti-medication. None of which is true.

I think the most important point for Cameron and his levels of medication is to try and find a balance between sufficient control of the psychotic thoughts and anxiety, balanced up against having sufficient alertness levels to be able to participate in life. If he takes a lot of medication to dull the psychosis, he becomes so sedated that he is unable to converse or concentrate and this impacts upon my quality of life with Cameron. Because we spend so much time at home together, I want to be able (and need) to have someone that actively participates in day-to-day activities, no matter how mundane they may be. Even a simple conversation and the ability to laugh or enjoy something together can be compromised if the sedation levels are too high. The flip side of this is, of course, that Cameron's quality of life is affected by the level of psychosis for which he needs his meds; insufficient medication means constant misery and anxiety and the inability to do anything at all. We both try to constantly stay alert to how he is coping with things. If we have had a busy week, then he may not feel so well and be exhausted from trying to keep his thoughts and actions together. If it has been a quieter week with less stress and less trips outside the house, he is likely to feel calmer and in control. This is a constant juggling game and activities must be planned in advance and monitoring of his coping is constant.

I have found it quite strange that CPNs would not want to include me in any discussions or, at the very least, invite me to join occasionally. I am the person who is with Cameron each and every day, and can give a report on how he has been in "my world" of non-psychosis. Cameron obviously needs to talk about "his world" and how he is coping with it, but I can give more objective information about alert levels, mood, motivation, tiredness. In the last few years, particularly when we were having sedation problems, I made a point of attending part of a meeting with a CPN. I thought it important to raise issues that "we" were facing as a couple. I often think that social/health services view the patient as an island, to be treated in isolation. There are many mental health sufferers who live alone, but many have family and it impacts on them, too. There are times when I feel that I am struggling to cope with things myself and it can get too much at times.

It is unfortunate that support workers and CPNs have to change regularly. It can take some time to get to know each other, to build a trusting relationship, and to feel more relaxed and able to open up and be yourself. Sometimes it feels that you are just getting to know one, then you are told they are moving to a different post and a new CPN will be in touch. Having a regular appointment provides stability and routine and these are so important, in my opinion, for staying on top of mental health issues. Visits to see the psychiatrist are less frequent and they are mostly local at our village surgery. Cameron attends these by himself and has one-to-one consultations. It can be very stressful if we have to go to Aberdeen for an appointment, but I do notice that Cameron relaxes immediately when we enter the mental health hospital grounds. It is as if he can just be himself because everyone in the environment knows what it is like to have a mental illness, or to work and support those who are ill. I think he feels safe there and that is why he relaxes.

When I still lived in Aberdeen, I used to use a drop-in centre in the middle of the city called National Schizophrenia Fellowship (NSF). It was a place where you could go and have a cup of tea. It was like a little sanctuary island in the middle of town, away from all the worry of all the other people watching you. You felt safe at the NSF. It was run by some paid staff and some volunteers. They ran out of funding and it closed many years ago. I used to find it a great comfort if I had to go into the city as I knew I could go there for a breather. Now, there is nowhere.

A list of helpful webpages and articles are listed in the Useful Webpages section at the back of the book.

CHAPTER 6
OUR LIFE TOGETHER

There are times when I reveal to a friend or colleague that my husband has schizophrenia and it is not long before they ask if I knew he was ill before we married, which I did. But I would like, at this point, to describe the man that I met and fell in love with. This happened before I knew about his illness. I have many very fond memories, as well as ones I would like to forget, from our life together. When I met Cameron, he was studying to be a primary school teacher. He is exceptionally good with children and can engage with them really well. I think it a shame that he was unable to complete his degree, as I feel he would be/is an excellent communicator with children. One of the traits he has for this is endless patience, which he most assuredly needs with me!

My enduring early memories of Cameron are of a gentle and very kind and generous man. It doesn't matter what you ask of Cameron, he will always give you more! I remember once asking him to go to the corner shop for cheese and he brought back about five packets (I still have the photo), and another occasion when he was making a sandwich and put a half packet of ham in it. I don't know if it was overcompensating, but he would always get you more, do more, give you more, just to be on the safe side! He has always been concerned with making you feel comfortable and putting your needs before his. He always opens a door for you, carries the shopping and has infinite patience, which makes him angelic! In the early years together, I thought he was handsome, intelligent, humorous and very kind. I had no idea that Cameron was ill. Even now, when people get to know Cameron, they are surprised at the lack of external indications of his illness and he is often described simply as being a little shy.

There have been some changes in Cameron's medication over the years, but for the last twenty or so he has been on clozapine. Although the dosage has changed, the medication has remained the same and Cameron is stable on it. Looking back, I can see there were gradual but significant changes in his levels of sedation. Because changes take place so gradually, you really don't seem to notice them.

There was a period of about eight to ten years where sedation really was a problem for me. In addition to simply being unable to hold a sensible conversation for any length of time because of lack of focus and concentration, I found it increasingly difficult to keep Cameron awake during the day. If he were to sit down on the sofa or comfy chair, he would be asleep in minutes. Not such a problem on its own, but this would happen several times a day and each day of the week. The biggest problem with falling sleep all the time was that one of the side effects of the medication is excess production of saliva. So, as Cameron dozed off, he would uncontrollably drool over whatever clothing he was wearing. I seemed to have the washing machine on continually. It drove me mad. Why couldn't he just stay awake? I told him that if he was going to have a seat, he should put a towel round his neck, so I could wash the towel, but he hated doing this. Not only did this happen at home all the time, but also when we were in the car driving anywhere where the journey was more than fifteen minutes. I would have one eye on the road and another to check if he were sleeping and if he had started drooling. Again, I would ask him to put something over his clothes, but he always refused, so we would arrive at our destination with a stain on his clothes. I really did find this *so* infuriating. A really simple thing to do to make my life a little easier, but he wouldn't do it.

Things started to get even worse when I was unable to wake Cameron when he had fallen asleep at home. I might have been out of the house, working or shopping, and I would return, and the doors were locked with the keys on the inside. I would knock and knock on the doors and windows and just not be able to rouse him at all. Again, I would get so angry about this. I learned that I would have to always have my house keys on my person and make sure that Cameron had not put his keys on the inside locks, otherwise I could be locked out for long enough. Even if I could gain entry to the house, I still could not wake him up. Cameron put on a lot of weight over the years – again, a side effect of the medication – and I was simply not strong enough to lift him up. I remember on several occasions literally yelling in his face to wake up and there would be no response. I found this very frightening. What if there were some emergency and I had to get him out of the house. I would be unable to do so. I also remember one occasion when I seemed to get him awake and he stood up and came at me, speaking gibberish. I realised that he was still sleeping, though walking and dreaming and talking.

On the second last day of the year, a few years ago, it got too much for me and I asked Cameron to make an appointment to see the psychiatrist, both of us together, so I could discuss how and why things had become so bad. It had got to the point where Cameron was sleeping while eating at the table, he was dropping cutlery and plates on the floor, and he couldn't hold a cup of tea without spilling it. His speech was increasingly slurred and indistinct. Something had to be done. The only thing that had changed in the previous six months was that Cameron had stopped smoking. The moment I told the psychiatrist this, she said that that was the reason for the excess sedation, because Cameron's liver was so much "cleaner" now, with less toxins in the body, so it was absorbing more medication. We then started on a journey of reducing medication and reviewing things regularly. I don't think we have quite found the perfect balance yet, but we were also referred to the sleep clinic for treatment of sleep apnoea and he now has a breathing machine to use when sleeping, which has made a massive difference to his levels of alertness as his body is receiving more oxygen.

In addition to problems with sleeping during the day, most of my married years have also had my nights plagued by Cameron sleepwalking. I think he has already related some of the instances when this was really problematic, such as being in the shower at three in the morning, or fully clothed while sleepwalking. Another time, I was woken in the morning by a loud thud and knew that he had fallen out of bed in his sleep. This was not quite accurate; he had fallen asleep standing up and fell into a door and dislocated his finger. So, we had to drive forty-five minutes to A&E. He had suffered from other injuries while falling in his sleep, to his elbow and leg. I found this to be very troublesome. I would wake up and Cameron would be asleep, but sitting on the edge of the bed, or walking around with all the lights on, or using the hairdryer, or opening the chest of drawers to get clothes out. He would even be sitting up, holding the telephone and chatting away in his sleep. I was worried every night when I went to bed that he would do something unsafe in his sleep. Simply getting out of bed as a sleepwalker is dangerous enough as you can fall at any time and Cameron was very overweight. But you might also fall onto furniture, damaging yourself, fall down the stairs, start cooking or putting lights on, or any number of things. Cameron has also been a very loud snorer. I ended up being such a light sleeper and with most nights spent awake or dozing, I was constantly exhausted during the day. This is not a great way for me to begin the day. I am a high energy person, but I give of my energies every day to my students and those I work with. How can I keep being the sole wage earner and do a professional job when I get no sleep at all? Things start to suffer.

The other main change that I have observed is Cameron's slow withdrawal into himself. As the years passed, he would be doing less around the house, engaging in conversation less, appearing less interested in things. There was a period of a few years when he would go trout fishing with a support worker. He really got into this pastime. He would make his own flies and spend hours making these intricate colourful objects. He enjoyed the guy's company and seemed to really like the whole fishing thing. Unfortunately, the worker moved on, as do many CPNs and support workers, and so the fishing interest died, too. It wasn't so much fun going alone, I suppose. Fishing and golf are the two main things that I have seen Cameron really enjoy. But over the years these have also fallen by the wayside, although he is now playing golf again.

In general terms, "our" life revolves around Cameron's needs. "My" life is mostly professional and although I have had a few friends that could be called "my friends", most are joint friends. Because of the issues Cameron has to deal with every day, it obviously has a massive impact on our shared living. One area where our needs overlapped was in my desire to start my own teaching practice, and for such a thing to happen we would need a detached property. This would also be better for Cameron's peace of mind in terms of having less intrusive effects from neighbours. Being self-employed and working from home would also mean spending more time together and working less hours. Our second home was semi-detached, but was suited very well to working downstairs and living upstairs. Unfortunately, the property had been poorly renovated and we were constantly plagued with problems. This is not an unusual situation, but when you are faced with being the sole wage earner, not getting any sleep and having to be the person to deal with all of the house issues – such as flooring not sitting on the joists, roof and road flooding, and fire from faulty wiring – you can understand that I found it all too much. I simply had to get rid of the house and find something that provided peace of mind for me (and for Cameron). I hoped it would also provide the opportunity to work from home.

Our next home looked like an excellent candidate. The neighbours were sufficiently far away, but we replaced the glazing with triple-glazing, just to be sure. During the first day of teaching from home, I could hear the next-door neighbour complaining about the noise. We seemed to have moved from one place of hell to another. How was I possibly going to be able to make a living and pay the mortgage if I had nowhere to work from? I ended up having to hire space, which ate into profits, but we both realised we would have to find a more suitable home as soon as possible (when finances allowed it). The locations of the previous two homes were wonderful, but were out-surpassed by our next and current home. This home is detached, with neighbours about 100 metres or so away. Most of the windows are facing our private garden and it has a double garage that is now converted into a teaching studio space. I thought this was the perfect house for both of us. I can work from home, so Cameron isn't left by himself for prolonged periods of time, and he has much more space around him for peace of mind. However, it seems that even with this in place, he still has issues with neighbours and traffic. I think we would have to live on an island with no planes overhead and no boats in the sea for Cameron to have peace in his head!

Socialising

Cameron finds quiet life at home a strain. Being in the garden, car or shop frightens him and causes immense anxiety. Socialising with people is almost impossible.

Good friends are very hard to come by. We both have had an enduring friendship with another couple, much our senior. I used to golf with him and we all smoked at the time. There was a lot of laughing and a lot of good times. We even went on holiday with them once. We used to play Trivial Pursuit and card games together. I think I got on so well with them because they were into singing and were empathetic with mental health needs. Unfortunately, they have now died. We have other good friends that can be relied upon and had some other good friendships in the past. A long-term friendship can be difficult to maintain as time passes. It is easy for friends to fall by the wayside, so it is important to try and keep them flourishing.

Over the years, we have had several very good friends. The better we know a friend, the easier it is to spend time with them. Having a meal at home with friends or family is usually the option we go for. Going out for a meal is a terrible strain for Cameron and me because I know from the outset that it is going to be difficult for him, so I try to make things comfortable for him from the moment we enter the restaurant. Where to sit is important and Cameron needs to make that decision. He will know the quietest place where he might attract the least attention. It is not uncommon to be offered a window seat in a restaurant or café, but that is the least attractive option for Cameron. All the passers-by will feed his psychotic thoughts and then this will be compounded by their ability to read his mind. He will always prefer to sit at the back in a corner. If the restaurant is busy, we turn away and go home.

There are many issues that cause problems when we eat out and, as such, I think we should do so only a few times in a year. The first thing is that the environment is unknown, so there are a lot of unfamiliar objects and people to have to negotiate. They might take Cameron's attention by surprise and so he is unprepared for the bad thoughts that come with them. We are also surrounded by many people who he thinks can read his thoughts and Cameron is constantly being drawn away from our conversation by the "babble" of chatter from other tables, because he thinks they are talking about him. It can be a real challenge to maintain Cameron's attention and focus. Every time we go to visit friends or family, I *always* say, "Please will you say something in the conversation?" It always ends up being me who does all the chatting and, believe it or not, I'm not that chatty a person and don't have much of interest to say. I think family and friends think that I bully Cameron or that I suppress him. When we are out socialising, he can go a whole meal and say about three words – even when I kick him under the table to say something, he would rather go home black and blue! It is difficult explaining this to people. It can easily be misinterpreted as lack of interest in those around him.

Like all other families, we get fed up eating my food all the time, especially as I haven't inherited culinary skills! I enjoy cooking and baking, especially now that I have more time, but I am not very good. Cameron recently remarked that my cooking was much better now than when we met. It has only been twenty-five years of practice! I would like to go out for romantic dinners with Cameron, but that isn't happening any time soon. So, we compromise and have takeout food instead. Fish and chips, yes please, and we both love Chinese and Indian cuisine.

When we are asked to attend a wedding, birthday or anniversary party, or even just a barbeque, we cannot do these things together. It is so difficult to say to someone that you cannot attend their wedding. How do you explain in a sentence the trauma that Cameron has to go through to attend a party? You can't. I sometimes make an excuse for both of us. If it is something that we really must attend, such as a funeral, Cameron will try and prepare himself for the ordeal and, if necessary, take some additional anxiety helping medication. There have been instances when I have attended a function by myself. This can be tricky because I worry that I have offended the host by coming alone. They may think that Cameron doesn't think highly enough of them to attend or is not supportive of me. Going to things by myself puts me under a bit of stress as I feel I have to justify why Cameron is not there, especially if we were both invited. And if I do go by myself, I usually spend most of the time worrying about Cameron and have to phone him to check-in with him to make sure he is okay.

For most of us, life is full of social celebrations and get-togethers. Times when we share in joy and sadness. For us, this does not happen or, at least, it does not happen easily or with much joy. If Cameron does attend an occasion, he will need a day or two to recover and I get very little sense or conversation during his quiet recovery time. Was the get-together worth it? Not for Cameron and probably not for me. Even the choosing of an appropriate birthday or greeting card can cause immense anxiety, as every image has connotations for Cameron. He has to buy his own Christmas cards as he needs to analyse the picture and verse to ensure they will not offend in any way. The same goes for wrapping paper. And writing a note or letter can take a very long time, as each and every word is laboured over to ensure they are the "right" words.

Leisure activities and entertainment

We do not really do leisure or entertainment. We try to go to the cinema once a year and it must be the first showing of the film on a Sunday, so it is the quietest time possible. Obviously, this is Cameron's choosing, not mine. Nothing like getting up early on a Sunday morning, having an hour's drive and trying to get yourself in movie mode by 11 in the morning! I can't remember the last time we went to a pub since we were students. Of course, Cameron doesn't drink due to the medications, but I make up for that. We also go to play the slot machines at the beach once a year. Again, this has to be first thing on a Sunday morning! These activities also need to be during school term time, as there are too many children going about during the holidays. I think Cameron finds psychotic thoughts about children the very worst to cope with, so he avoids any times when there are likely to be children about. This means that we do not go shopping during the school lunch break, for example.

It is possible to go to the cinema. I have a four-point plan:

1) Wait until at least two weeks after the film comes out, so that the initial scramble to see it is over.
2) Go on a Sunday as this will be the quietest day with the least amount of people.
3) Go to the first showing of the day, preferably before noon. This is likely to be the quietest time of the day.
4) When buying your ticket, ask the ticket seller to give you a seat in the back row and way off to one side.

This is my best chance to enjoy the film, as it doesn't get much quieter than going early on a Sunday morning. Following these few rules, I've been to watch films where there was seating for about 200 people, but there were only a handful of people in the auditorium. I really enjoy it when that happens.

I am trying to think what other leisure activities we have done together, but am struggling. I sometimes read a book to Cameron, but he does not read himself as he cannot concentrate on the content. I have tried to get Cameron walking, but that is stressful because of other pedestrians and traffic. We sometimes walk up the hill behind our house. If you walk for long enough, you can go over the top and not see houses anymore. I can see him visibly relaxing at this point and I think there is some enjoyment experienced. His face relaxes and he talks more. He is more observant and smiles at the rabbits running around and the colours on the hills. When I focus on the difficulties that Cameron faces every moment, it makes me so deeply sad and I wish I could do something to make life more of a joy for him instead of a struggle.

Because we cannot go out for socialising and entertainment, we tend to stay in and entertain ourselves. We both have a passion for sci-fi and for music. Almost all of the time while at home, Cameron will have music playing. Since discovering technology a couple of years ago, after my nagging him to get into the 21st century, he listens to YouTube now. I do not listen to music for leisure as my ears find it very difficult to switch off. I spend all day in my professional life listening and giving feedback on music performances. I think Cameron finds music soothing and a distraction. We watch films and series together and have enjoyed doing box sets of Star Trek (all series) several times over the years. I think that Cameron likes to have a really engaging film that forces his attention to activate, as this is most distracting for him. I am not sure that he "enjoys" a film, as he always has a commentary running through his head and can struggle with ideas of reference. I know that he often does not follow the story and misses sections of films or programmes. There is nothing more annoying than watching TV and being subjected to a barrage of questions about who that is, what is going on, where did he come from, etc.

I have been on holiday about five times in the last twenty-five years. What you have to bear in mind is that when you go on holiday, you take your problems with you. I once naïvely thought I would leave all the troubles behind. My last holiday to Mexico City was the toughest two weeks I have ever experienced. We went to visit Tara's dad, who lives there. It is not so bad if a relative is driving you everywhere and you are going for meals in groups of four. Then, you don't feel you are the main focus, just part of the group. For reference, remember that I am constantly thinking that people are talking about me and I react in a way that reinforces the delusion. I am thinking these strangers can read my mind. All loud noises affect me, put me down and reinforce my negative thoughts. The volume of traffic in the city is unbelievable and that is compounded by its noise. Every moment of this holiday was so severely painful. I thought I was going to die for fourteen continual days. It has scarred me for life and I am still nursing the wounds. The city you choose for a holiday is so important to your experience. We found Warsaw to be really nice: peaceful yet beautiful, as are the people. For me, a group of four is better than a group of two, as delusions and phobias affect me less.

My first holiday, which was in a group of four, decades ago, had me getting up at four in the morning to catch a plane. The sound of the engines at the end of the walkway tunnel was becoming louder and louder and when I reached the plane, the sound was deafening. My first reaction was, "No, I'm not getting on this plane!" The noise was so overwhelming, and in the next split second, I realised I would spoil everyone's holiday if I didn't get on the plane. I just said to myself, "You have to go, whatever." I got on the plane and nearly blacked out with stress on take-off. For me, planes are disturbing and upsetting.

The longer the holiday, the more it takes it out of me. Shorter holidays are more manageable. On a longer holiday, you are a long way from home if something goes wrong, with every second hurting you. When I went to Mexico, I lost the ability to speak coherently as a direct result of stress. My delusions had kicked in hard and I was frequently crying, and I thought I was going to die. I was so frightened, so intensely, for so long.

I've been too frightened for the past few decades to go to a pub to socialise or just to have lunch with Tara, as I am always worried about trouble. On holiday, you must eat out and be out of the hotel all the time. You must learn how to cope with the "uncopeable". The only advice I can give myself is that I need to really plan ahead to my specific needs. You must not prolong being in pain. Don't give your delusions room to manoeuvre, otherwise they take complete control and upset everyone concerned.

I cannot say I have yet enjoyed a holiday with Cameron. It does not seem to matter how much we try and plan and accommodate his needs, it is still traumatic. If we are away, just the two of us, I can only go out and about when Cameron feels well enough. Usually that will mean one outing a day, but sometimes, no outings. An outing will perhaps be to have our evening meal in a restaurant. If we are to eat out, we cannot also go out and visit something the same day. If we decide to go shopping, we have to stay in the hotel room for dinner. We have frequently had to have room service because it is too much stress to go to a café local to the hotel for a meal, and even having a meal in the hotel can bring on an anxiety attack. If we visit a gallery, we will not be able to go out again that day. If one event was too traumatic, Cameron will need a day to recover in the hotel room. It goes without saying, choosing the hotel itself is vitally important as we have to spend so much of our holiday time in it. We have discovered that if there is sound-proofing, it helps alleviate a lot of additional stress for Cameron, so this is one of the first things we look for in the hotel amenities list.

If we are in a safe place, with wide open spaces, I might go out by myself, but not far. What is the point of travelling to other places, even if it is only a few miles away from home, if you cannot get out and explore? Simply sitting in the sun outside our hotel is fine for me, but Cameron will then be in the hotel room worrying about my safety when I am not with him in the hotel room. So I can stay in the hotel room with him being really miserable, go out myself and make him miserable, or we can go out together and all Cameron will say is, "When are we going back to the hotel?"

Holidays are problematic. So, of course, we are back to the dilemma I wrote about earlier. I can go on holiday by myself or I can go on holiday with friends, but I think holidays with Cameron are unlikely to be very successful, even if they are as short as possible! And then when I leave him at home, I am guilty that he is not with me; that I am having fun and he is not. Then, I worry that friends think it strange that I have gone away without him. Then, while away, I need to stay in touch with him all of the time to make sure he is okay and to reassure him that I am okay. I am exhausted just thinking about it!

Accommodating each other

Dealing with Cameron's OCD drives me bananas! I sometimes try to ignore it, but most of the time I just explode. Even if I check switches and taps for him, he still goes to check them. What is the point of both of us doing it? Can he not take my word for it? I can check everything in a minute or less, but Cameron will take a long time. It is such a waste of time. I sometimes go into the loo after him simply so he will not have to check everything and I will do it for him, otherwise each visit to the loo can take ages. I am very frustrated most of the time as I try to reason with Cameron about his actions, which is, of course, futile. What seems perfectly obvious to me is very problematic for him. I sometimes make attempts to convince Cameron of something or have a logical conversation about an aspect that is troubling him (and troubling me), but it is pointless. You cannot reason with a brain that, in Cameron's words, suffers from "faulty wiring".

There are many things that are different for me as I adjust things in life, so they are more manageable for Cameron. For example, if we go somewhere in the car and he will be waiting in the car while I do the shopping or have a rehearsal, I am instructed where to park the car. We frequently have arguments about whether his priorities are more important than mine. I might want to park in the shade to keep the contents of the car cool, but we cannot park there because there is another car next to us, or the front windows are looking onto houses. It seems to be a constant battle of wills. But, of course, it is not. Most of the time I am simply being uncaring and unthoughtful; I am putting myself first. Does it really matter where the car is parked and if the cheese gets sweaty?! Let's face it, given the daily challenges that Cameron has to deal with, it really is unimportant. I think the reason we (I should say, I) have mini battles of will is simply because most of the time I "forget" that Cameron has schizophrenia. I don't mean that I deliberately forget. I mean that, if I had to constantly remind myself of the horrors in his head, I don't think I could function. I attempt to get on with life with as little disruption as possible and part of that involves me almost "blocking out" awareness of his difficulties sometimes. One of us needs to be able to cope and function adequately.

I am a creative sort and, as a teacher, usually have a fair amount of patience. If I have been asked the same question for the third time in the space of some minutes, I start to get a bit edgy. Cameron does have problems retaining simple pieces of information or instructions. It is as if the first "telling" simply slips by in the ether; words were said and heard, but not retained as their decibels diminish. Cameron has said himself that there is a problem with things *registering* in his brain; it takes more focus and concentration for it to be preserved with its meaning and then acted upon. This happens all the time and I lose my patience and raise my voice or slam a door. This then causes anxiety for Cameron as he associates noise with the intensity of the psychotic thoughts he is experiencing. So, a simple strategy for me is to encourage Cameron to write things down, then he does not have to try and remember anything. Will he do it? Will he heck!

Cameron, in general, is much more stable in terms of mood than me. I know what I will get most days from Cameron. If something upsets me, I will say what it is that upsets me. People who know me know that I don't hold back when it comes to speaking my mind. I cannot abide any strife, anxiety or worry; it literally makes me feel ill in the pit of my stomach. I must deal with the problem, do what I can and then there is no point worrying about it as it is out of my control. I like to clear the air as soon as possible. Cameron is uncommunicative when it comes to essentials. I can always tell when I have accidentally upset him as he will not say anything at all – no light conversation is to be had in the slightest. He clams up and waits for me to acknowledge my error. The problem with this approach is that most of the time I am oblivious to the thing I am supposed to have done or said. This comes back to mind-reading, I think. Cameron thinks that I know what he is thinking, so he does not need to verbalise the issue. He is simply waiting patiently for my response or apology. If I ask what the problem is, he will either say there is nothing wrong or say that I know what is wrong. And when I reply that I do not know, he cannot accept that answer and goes back into his quiet zone until I repent. This is another of those frustrating events. When it happens, I sometimes see him looking at me with disdain and disgust, and can almost see him having psychotic thoughts by the way he looks at me. Fortunately, this happens infrequently.

Cameron accepts that he is too sensitive and sometimes takes a throwaway comment of mine too literally and it hurts him. I must accept and realise more profoundly that all I say and do is filtered through his brain and translated into disturbing, irrational thoughts and ideas. While my side of a conversation may seem banal, it may not be received that way once it arrives in Cameron's mind. This concept can affect the level of conversation that I have with Cameron. If I can sense that he is less well, or less able to cope, then I will either make occasional light conversation as a distraction, or the safer option is to say nothing. This reduces my ability to interfere with his perceptions as I have removed the verbal stimulus and am left only with my behaviours. Behaviours may still be "misread", but I am less likely to upset him if I say nothing.

The essentials of our life are all done by me. Cameron did used to drive but gave up his license about twenty years ago as he felt he couldn't trust his judgement. He was a much better driver than me. Any medical appointments will require me taking him there. Any leisure activities, such as golf, will also need me to drive him there. I don't mind doing these things at all; that is what a marriage is all about. There is the odd time when I am unable to take Cameron somewhere and he will have to get a taxi. Cameron has not been on a bus or train for decades. Almost any job that needs done in life has to be done by me. There are a few things Cameron will do such as change a fuse in a plug, do the dishes, hoover, make the bed and fold up washing. He will not use the iron. He struggles in the garden to help and can't even get any enjoyment from sitting in the garden because of his thoughts. I think he does like looking out at the garden from the safety of indoors, though, and watching the antics of the birds and other wildlife. I thought it would be great in our current home to sit outside together, but it is not to be.

I'm so glad that Tara can see the fact that I have no motivation to do anything. It is easily the biggest of my problems and affects every single issue in my life. Many, many people do not, for one reason or another, see the impact no motivation can have on an outcome. Be it that they may not realise I have schizophrenia, or they may know precious little about the illness. It's better in the long term if everyone knows. Sometimes it's a relief when they know you have the illness, otherwise you can easily be categorised as someone quite negative. I think Tara copes extremely well when it comes to my limitations. It's a whole cacophony of thoughts and emotions: embarrassment, anger, upset,

gratefulness, shamefulness, thankfulness, feeling guilty and feeling very sad. I
generally suffer a lot of upset.

I try hard not to fail her, so if a job is really beyond me, I'll try to make
the situation a little better by doing a job a little less demanding on me, but
something that will help the situation. I can't mow the garden because of
psychotic thoughts about neighbours and people reading my mind. I don't want
the neighbours to know I have psychotic thoughts about them, over which I have
no control. The spontaneous interaction between me mowing and my neighbours
leaves me with a feeling that is bitterly inappropriate and highly inexcusable. So,
to help Tara, I might do the dishes instead or some other job in the house like
hoovering. I can do less harm if I stay in the house.

I know that Cameron feels bad that he can't do more to help me.
I am not sure how to help him feel less inadequate. There are
many times when I ask him to help with something that requires
two people and he might, but frequently he will say that he doesn't
feel well enough. Usually I just don't ask for help, unless it is a
task I am unable to do by myself. This translates into my life as
stubbornness, I think. I am so used to having to do everything
myself that I do not expect others to help and I do not ask for
help. Most of the time, I accept my role and get on with things,
but there are days when I have had enough of doing everything
all the time. I am already responsible for bringing in a salary and
providing a professional service to all of my students, and then I
must be responsible for everything in the home and garden, too.
It can get too much for me. If I have a big gardening job to do, I
might wait until Cameron goes golfing because then I can do the
job and not worry about him sitting in the house watching me do
it, feeling guilty and ashamed. I find it can help him if I "hide"
the jobs I have needed to do, or try and get them done as quickly
and with as little complaining as possible. Life must continue,
things need to be done, but I don't want to add to his distress.
Doing tasks causes Cameron a lot of anxiety and fear and *not*
doing tasks causes him to feel guilty.

Although Cameron has not prepared or cooked a meal for
decades, he will help me with meals and he is an excellent maker of

tea and coffee! All the bottles and jars in the kitchen have the top turned too tightly and I can never get them off. I keep asking him to put the tops of bottles on less securely so I can get them off, but he can't. It is the same with door handles and the wood stove handle – anything that has to be closed. Thinking he is doing a good job by having it really secure, it ends up that the top gets broken. I don't ask Cameron to do the wood stove anymore, as I worry that he will break the door handle. Simple things cause frustration.

It is almost impossible for us to make a spontaneous decision to do something as Cameron likes to prepare himself for everything. I don't mind too much as my professional life involves a lot of activity and mixing with people. I am mostly glad to be quiet at home. I think what I miss most is the strength and support you have in a life partner – those times when I need to be carried along because I don't feel so great. Or those times when your partner suggests doing something or makes the decisions for you. Cameron's endless understandable pessimism can be draining and I do not always have the strength to cope well. I seem to go through highs and lows in terms of how well I cope. I find that when I am busy, it is easier for me as my mind is busy with projects, people and planning. One of our most difficult times was when the coronavirus hit the UK at the start of 2020.

CHAPTER 7
DEALING WITH THE CORONAVIRUS PANDEMIC

At the start of 2020, our ways of living changed. We were all facing an unseen foe, ever-present and threatening. Covid-19 started in Wuhan and gradually spread across the globe. It travelled quickly to the UK with a hotspot in London and before we knew what was happening, we all had to Stay Home, Protect the NHS and Save Lives.

The first couple of weeks of staying at home felt like being in a state of limbo. How long will this be for? Is it really as bad as news reporting suggests? Will it all blow over soon? I tried to fill my time with knitting, doing jigsaws and watching TV. It was a strange experience, seeing and hearing about the spread of the virus and its destructive effects, while we were both in a safe bubble at home, having a "home holiday" or "staycation".

As the weeks passed, it became apparent that this way of life was to continue for some period of time. I had to try and find a routine that I could follow for my own sanity. There were obvious financial concerns about the inability to work, so I researched software and applications that might help me to deliver music lessons online, and also allow Banchory Singers community choir to continue rehearsing. The UK government provided financial support, but I still wanted to keep students and choir members active and maintain a connection with them. Many choir members were shielding, so they were always to stay at home. For these people, I thought that some online group meetings would be helpful and lift spirits during this challenging, often depressing, time for everyone.

After a few experimental rehearsals using the Zoom app, I managed to settle into a way of creating multitrack recordings that I could share at the rehearsal meetings so members could sing along. Before this, I would play and sing live, but this did not simulate a choir rehearsal where you hear all voice parts at the same time. And, of course, we could not all sing live together because of the time delay with the technology. We met twice a week to rehearse and chose uplifting songs to help keep our spirits up. Some students wished to try online lessons and others recorded performances for feedback. My way of working was completely online now, with no face-to-face contact. This provided me with a focus and helped to keep me sane and to feel that I was positively contributing.

Our home routine changed only a little. We went out shopping as infrequently as possible. I was providing some support for my mum once every two weeks, which involved a 100-mile round trip. Cameron would come with me in the car on these trips, but we were effectively leaving the house less than before the stay at home rule. This suited Cameron better, as he didn't have to be outside as much. But when we were outside, there were significantly less people about as everyone was in lockdown and discouraged to leave their homes. So, streets and food supermarkets were quieter, but also very eerie. There was a one-way system to follow in the shop, you must keep physically distanced from people and everyone was wearing face masks. There was a feeling of being on edge, ensuring you do and say the correct things. The old rules of how to go about your daily lives were rewritten. You had to learn a new set of rules for social behaviour and interactions. Not everyone knew all these rules or were sure how to implement them. Simple shop visits or walking down a pavement had new procedures to be followed. Nothing felt the same and the uncertainty of your own actions made you quite stressed. You could see in the action and movement of others their own insecurities. Everyone was struggling.

Other things at home were fairly similar from a practical perspective, but I found my mental state was fragile. The constant bombardment on the television about the virus was persistent to the point of obsession. After a few weeks, I decided we had to limit ourselves to only watching the news at certain times of the day as we were both getting caught up in the media frenzy and it made me unable to function effectively. I also felt guilty staying at home and not working while key workers were working incredibly hard and under huge pressures and threats to their health. Each day, we would watch the number of deaths from coronavirus going up, and even when they plateaued and started to come down, they came down very slowly. Each day seemed to be filled with negativity. Due to the inability of governments to give dates for things going back to "normal" because of the threat of Covid-19, this state of limbo continues. I find that my mental health has suffered tremendously in this time. The possibility of "normal" returning is unlikely for some time. I find the uncertainty the main challenge to my state of mind.

There have also been boredom factors to contend with. Boredom of looking at the same walls, the same faces, doing the same tasks each day, the same conversations and the same voices being heard. I might give myself plenty to do, but that does not mean I am not bored. My brain needs a little more variety to keep it functioning well. I am sure I am not alone in this. Finding things to occupy the mind as a distraction have been fundamental for me.

Cameron has become quite obsessed with keeping up to date with the latest statistics of deaths from Covid-19, here and abroad. I became aware that when the news was on the television, he was getting more agitated the longer it was showing, so I would shut it off. He spends a lot of time on his tablet, some of which I hope is a distraction for him. He seems to have had much less patience with me (and I with him) and has had a couple of outbursts. I have had many outbursts. Everything has been fraying at the seams. He has been much more anxious and physically agitated and the speed at which he talks has increased. His speaking is edgy and a little frantic.

The coronavirus pandemic has subtly pushed me over the safe line. Before the virus, there was some fashion of containment, but not now. I feel as though I have lost about a third of my ability to cope with everyday things.

T   What is it about the virus pandemic that has had this effect on you?

C   Increased worrying and more fear.

T   More fear about what?

C   Am I going to catch the virus? Am I going to die? What if I transmit it to someone else and I don't know? What can I do to help?

T   What precautions have you been taking to protect yourself and others?

C   I have not been visiting anybody. I stay two metres away from everyone.

T   What about hand washing?

C   Oh yeah, I do plenty of that.

T   Hand washing has been a bit obsessive, yes?

C   I suppose so.

T   So, if you take precautions, it is unlikely you will catch the virus or pass it on. Is there more you think you could be doing?

C   No, I don't think so.

T   So you are being as safe as you can be?

C   Yes, I think so.

T   Does this make you feel safer? Does it make you worry less?

C   Not really. I already have loads of fear and it is just compounded now.

When I am out of the house, I can see the fear in people about catching Covid-19 and almost smell the fear of those around me. With all the fear going on, it is difficult to act normal and be objective. It puts more pressure on people to function as normal. People used to get through things somehow before. Now, everyone is in unchartered waters and they are struggling to cope under increased pressure. People are getting stressed out. You can even see it with newsreaders on the TV. Everyone is finding it hard to keep it together.

I isolate myself most of the time, as my preferred option, but with the coronavirus, people are struggling to isolate for just a few months. Being out and about for me must be worse than regular people having to stay at home and isolate. I can easily cope with isolation. I haven't seen my support worker, CPN or psychiatrist for months. Mentally ill people need their help now, especially considering the way things have been unfolding. I am definitely right on the precipice.

T   What do you feel you need from mental health services just now?

C   Some help rationalising it all.

T   Do I not help with that?

C   Yes you do.

T   So, you feel you need another pair of ears, a different perspective?

C   I am just fed up hearing about the same stuff every day.

The same loop of deaths and statistics. I have nothing to look forward to in terms of golfing with the support worker. I just feel all alone, you know.

T   What do you mean, all alone?

C   I just feel hopeless.

T   Can you expand?

C   I feel nearer to death.

T   Do you mean from catching the virus?

C   Yes. Just the increased physical risk of catching the virus and dying. There is a definite increase in the risk of dying over the next few months. People are shopping wearing sci-fi suits, all wrapped up in white paper boiler suits and face masks.

T   Do you find face masks intimidating?

C   I find them worrying. Especially when I am at the doctor's for my blood tests. I am not allowed to touch the door handle, I have to use hand sanitiser, put on a mask, sit in a seat that is isolated from everyone else. It is like military style procedures, like in a sci-fi. It is a real eye-opener. Then, you wonder if you are in the process of catching coronavirus after all that. So, I am paranoid about touching surfaces and picking up the virus.

T   So is it your own life you are worried about or being an unknown transmitter?

C   Both.

Since the coronavirus, my outward flapping of my arms when I am out in public has a new, deteriorated, uncontrollable element. I feel that I am not in control enough. For me, at the moment, the slightest of things feels extremely dangerous and catastrophic. I am mentally disturbed by fear, fear, fear. When I am at the checkout when shopping, I'm getting in an uncontrollable state to the point of borderline incoherency. My behaviour deteriorates and I can't speak normally. The coronavirus pandemic has simply put another level of fear on top of the layers I already have.

You don't realise how important family are until you can't see them. Thank God I've been able to phone my mum and speak to her. It puts a different perspective on things when you know you can't see them. Not being able to go into hospital or visit relatives in care homes is shocking. It is cruel. I don't know how people manage. They are braver than me.

A silver lining

We are still living through the coronavirus pandemic. I am unsure how things will turn out. We are all learning to live with the threat and adjust to a new normal. However, one good thing has come from all of this. I had begun to really worry about Cameron's physical health as he was staying inside, as we all were, far too much, and not getting any physical exercise or fresh air. I was getting out and doing lots of walking, but being outside is just too stressful for Cameron, so I walked alone. As I mentioned earlier, I succeeded in persuading him to walk up the hill behind our house and that seemed to be quite pleasurable for him, but we have since discovered the Haughton Park in the village and now go there almost every day.

Walking in a woodland park might not sound like the most inspirational of activities, but it has changed "our" life together. This is the first time in our lives when we can both do an outdoor activity and get some enjoyment from it. I just love to walk and am a country girl at heart, so really enjoy the changing colours, sights and sounds of the woods. But it is doubly pleasurable because I have my husband by my side, walking hand in hand through the mud. The coronavirus pandemic has encouraged everyone to socialise outdoors as the open air is a safer environment and avoids its spread. We have seen lots of people take up walking, jogging and cycling: it really is a time for outdoor pursuits.

So, given all of Cameron's anxiety in being outside, how have we succeeded in walking in the woods most days? Simply put, the woodland and paths are extensive, and the tree cover is dense. There is a wide range of paths from the wide ones regularly used by dog walkers, cyclists and runners, and there are much less used paths that meander through the undergrowth. This means that we can take less used paths and we are less likely to see other people because of the bushes and trees. It took us many visits to get a mental map of where all the tracks go, and which were quieter and less frequented. Cameron also insists that we go at a time of day when there are likely to be less people going about. So, this means we usually go at mealtimes. Living in the north of Scotland we have had wonderful daylight hours over the summer months for teatime walks, but as autumn has come in and the evening light is much less, we have changed to lunchtime walks. So, while most people are at home, we are out and about in the woodland park.

Cameron still has anxiety in getting to the park as we need to drive there, and we do sometimes meet people on the paths which disturbs his thinking and hence his enjoyment. For most of the time we enjoy each other's company, see lots of wildlife including birds, deer, red squirrels and rabbits; we hear the sounds of the wind and rain and rustling of the leaves. We have had the pleasure of watching the wild-flower field blossom and die away, seen the heron fishing in the Don, and watched the rise and fall of the river level. We have smelled the damp leaves and watched the forest change on each visit. Such a simple thing has given me immense joy because we do it together and he seems to enjoy it. We are also getting the added benefits of oxygenated blood, increased heart rate, and building up muscle strength, so it has helped us both mentally and physically. What a joy!

I asked Cameron to share his thoughts about our almost daily walks and he was unable to move beyond obsessing about the trauma of meeting people and the psychotic thoughts he has to deal with. I was hoping he could focus on the positive aspects of our walks together, as he does appear to enjoy them, he even smiles and visibly relaxes. This just emphasises the power of mental illness and its hold over the mind, attitudes, and emotions.

T   Tell me something of how it is for you to go walking in the park.

C   I find it really difficult to be torn away from the house in the first place. It is so traumatic being outside and I feel safer at home.

T   But you have been going walking for some months now, so there must be something positive in the experience?

C   When I get home, I can register the benefit of it, once I am home and safe.

T   So while we are in the park you do not get any joy from it?

C   Well, the odd moment. But everything is traumatic outside.

T   So if there are no people going about, why is it still traumatic for you?

C   Because I think they can hear us speaking.

T   But if there are no people about, how can they hear you if they are not there?

C   If we can hear them, then they can hear us.

T   How often do we see and/or hear other people?

C   Not that often.

T   On a walk we have frequently had no encounters with anyone at all, and if we do, I think it would have been no more than maybe four encounters at the most in one walk. In between these meetings are you not able to relax with me and enjoy the sights, sounds and smells of the woods at all?

C   A little bit.

T   Is there anything positive about the experience that you can share at all, rather than fixating on the negative aspects of having to deal with meeting other people?

C   There are little snippets where if I see the squirrel running through the branches or see a bunny, it is really cute seeing these things. It is a welcome distraction.

T   I think it is a wonderful experience to see nature and wildlife in their own habitat. I feel privileged to observe it and feel part of it.

C   When I see the wildlife it is the highlight of the walk. But when I am in the woods I am constantly looking for where the next person is coming from.

T   Do you mean that during the whole time we are in the park, you are anticipating meeting someone, so it hampers your ability to relax and enjoy your time outside?

C   Uh-huh. The threat level is high.

T   Even when we meet no one?

C   Yes, I am just in a state of fear.

T   So you don't get much joy from it?

C   I do like looking at the sky through the branches.

And there is the silver lining: fleeting moments of pleasure that I have observed in Cameron, and that he acknowledges, in among all the anxiety and fear. It brings me some comfort that he can glimpse tiny moments of joy and recognises the benefits when back home in his safe zone. And I love spending this precious time with him.

Coping strategies

I have attended different meetings in the past to discover helpful coping strategies for my illness. Nothing materialised. About a year ago, I asked my psychiatrist for a list of coping strategies. She said she would look into it.

Shortly afterwards, she was promoted and that was the end of the strategy list for me. I have come up with my own list of strategies after lots of trial and error. I think this is the best way for an individual to find what works for them.

a) One day at a time. Don't let things get you down. Break the workload of dealing with the illness into daily amounts. Just deal with today.

b) Saying prayers when outside, but inside your head, silently. When things are absolutely hopeless, I get some comfort by just saying my prayers for as long as I need to.

c) Back to basics. If being heavily scrutinised by people, just go back to the basics of things being either right or wrong without added complications. Whatever I say or do is either right or wrong. If it is right, then keep doing it; if it is wrong, stop it before it goes further.

d) Favourite song and all the lyrics. I obtain the lyrics for my favourite song and just sing it to myself silently in my head when out and about or at home. It distracts me and raises my mood.

e) How in heaven? If feeling acute trauma, I say to myself, "How would they do this in heaven?" An example of this is when I put the bins out on the roadside, I would try and do this gracefully, with a pleasant mood, not banging about, and in a way that would generate an uplifting mood.

f) Buying a present. I think of buying presents for people. Who am I buying it for, and what am I buying and why? It distracts me and raises my mood because I feel good when I give someone a gift.

g) Focus on breathing out for longer than it takes to breathe in. This helps lessen psychotic intensity.

h) At home 99 per cent. Being at home for the vast majority of the week is a comforting thought when compared to being outside. If I am outside and I say this to myself, at least it is less than *one per cent a week of exposure. This puts perspective on the levels of suffering endured and breaks the pain up into more manageable portions.*

CHAPTER 8
THE WAY AHEAD

I have been trying to write this book for many years now. I take a shot at it maybe once a year. Without motivation, it is a tall order. Nevertheless, I am writing now. I can see how I've developed over the years in how I write. The learning curve of life makes you better and more knowledgeable and a more rounded individual. My ability to think has improved year on year, for which I am pleased. Everything changes and you need to constantly rethink and change your perspective. You are always adapting your thoughts.

T   What have you learned from writing this book?

C   There are lots of answers we do not have yet.

T   In relation to what?

C   Finding the best medication and doses. All I think about all the time is about being well. That means I think about medication a lot.

T   That doesn't answer my question. Have you not got any observations from the processes of writing and talking together as we have worked on this project?

C   (Silence.)

T   For example, how easy have you found it to articulate what you experience, and to put things into words? Has it been difficult? Has it been emotional?

C   It has been difficult to focus on all the problems. Opening up old wounds is hard.

T   These wounds are still with you today?

C   Yes, but they have been there a long time. That is what I meant by old wounds.

T   Is there anything else you want to share about what it has been like writing the book?

C   It has been nice to think that the odd thing I have written might be helpful to others. Hopefully, we can give them things to think about. I have tried to point out things that I have done wrong so others might learn from it.

T   Is there anything that you have learned about our relationship from writing together?

C   I maybe haven't given enough time to your point
      of view.
T   Have you been surprised when I have not understood what
      you were trying to say in your writing?
C   Yes, there have been a few times. It is difficult to
      articulate something that is abstract without making
      yourself too ill.

*Here are some of my reflections after completing writing this book. I have
had to re-examine some old wounds in the process of writing, which I found
painful. I have found it better to speak about these things than to leave
them unscrutinised. I have become more aware of the intrusive nature of
schizophrenia in this process and that is very disturbing. It is difficult to be
precise when you are dealing with such an abstract concept – thought is such
a delicate thing that you don't want to take a sledgehammer to it. I found
self-examination hard work and have discovered some things that I would
have preferred to have stayed hidden, such as how dark the illness is. I have
found comfort in the idea that if you are mentally ill, you are meant to have
these thoughts. One way of viewing the illness is that it is random brain
activity and this also brings me comfort. I have learned for myself that ideas
of reference and no motivation are my two most debilitating hurdles. Positives
that I have taken away from this process are to be happier at home and things
are always changing and evolving, and I am always learning and growing.*

I have found writing this book with Cameron something of a
trial at times. Because Cameron is not motivated, it has been very
hard to keep him on track and do some writing about what it is
like living with this illness. Although I have been the main writer,
I have tried to keep Cameron's words exactly as he wrote or said
them. Reading over pages of his handwriting, trying to articulate
the world that is inside his head, is not easy. Sometimes, it feels
like reading an exploding emotion. The words do not necessarily
form well-drafted sentences, but the feeling of fear and lack of
control is palpable beneath the words.

In the early days working on the text, I learned a lot about
what was going on in Cameron's mind that I did not know before.

My first feeling was one of shock at what he experiences all day every day and that I had not known these things. How could we be married for such a long time and I only now realise that I don't really know my husband at all? Then I would feel immense sadness that an individual has to carry this awful burden with him constantly. The only respite is when sleeping. Not being in control of your own thoughts and dealing with the fear and anxiety of people being able to read your mind is incomprehensible. We have focused on the illness and its effects and there has been a lot of negative and unsettling issues uncovered. While our life together has its difficulties, it must be said that we do quite a lot of laughing together, too. This has not always been reflected in our storytelling.

During this process of learning about each other I have felt a lot of guilt. Guilt that my life is so much easier than his. Guilt that I do not support Cameron as much as I could and should. Guilt that I make him do things that he doesn't want to do. I have also learned that my ability to be objective is not to be taken for granted. I can see things from different angles, weigh up options and make the best decisions. I do not have an illness that I can use to blame my poor judgement on. I should be a better person than I am because I do not have all these mental issues hampering my thinking.

I realise now, after rereading this book, that I have not once referred to myself as Cameron's carer. Why have I not recognised this role? In a marriage, it is a partnership of responsibilities. I think I can see that our partnership contains three entities: me, Cameron and the beast that lives in his head. Cameron is unable to make objective decisions, his judgement cannot always be relied upon and he cannot always provide the support I – or he – needs. Equally, I know I often fall short of providing the support that he needs. But the important part is that we each do what we can for each other. I simply have to do more, much more, so I suppose it is time to accept that I do care for Cameron and he would not function so well without me. That is also a worry.

As a result of learning of all the challenges that Cameron faces each day, I am left with a dilemma. Do I simply change all that we do so as to protect him from additional stress? Do we stay at home with as little contact with the outside world as possible? These measures may help to alleviate some of the symptoms of the illness, but do they add to a quality of life? In what ways can I be supportive of him without losing my own sense of self? What adjustments can be made so as to improve quality of life for Cameron without me losing mine? How can we each live a life together where potential is achieved and we can each flourish?

T   What is a good quality of life for you?

C   Being in control of my thoughts.

T   What about activities or things you can do that could give you a sense of happiness or achievement?

C   Being accepted gives me a sense of happiness. My dream is to walk down the pavement and be deep in my own healthy thoughts.

T   So having a good quality of life does not involve particular activities or meeting people or friends?

C   Dignity is important. As long as there is dignity.

I hope that this book gives you some idea of the nature of living with schizophrenia. I have written about my life. I have tried to point out a few of my mistakes along the way that may help you.

I hope my future will be like this:

- I will be happier when I spend time at home. Home is where I am in least pain, so I should be happier there.
- I hope I continue to grow out of my illness.
- I hope to rationalise my thinking more. It is one of the few tools at my disposal.
- I hope to understand the shortcomings of my illness with a view to improving myself and how I interact with others.
- I will smile a lot more in the future.

USEFUL WEBPAGES

www.activemeditation.org
www.betterhelp.com
www.headspace.com
www.livingwithschizophreniauk.org
www.mind.org.uk
www.nhs.uk/conditions/schizophrenia
www.nhs.uk/conditions/stress-anxiety-depression/mindfulness/
www.petsastherapy.org
www.rethink.org
www.samh.org.uk
www.shawmind.org
www.verywellmind.com
www.wikipedia.org

ABOUT CHERISH EDITIONS

Cherish Editions is a bespoke self-publishing service for authors of mental health, wellbeing and inspirational books. As a division of Trigger Publishing, the UK's leading independent mental health and wellbeing publisher, we are experienced in creating and selling positive, responsible, important and inspirational books, which work to de-stigmatise the issues around mental health and improve the mental health and wellbeing of those who read our titles.

Cherish Editions is unique in that a percentage of the profits from the sale of our books goes directly to mental health charity Shaw Mind, to deliver its vision to provide support for those experiencing mental ill health. Find out more about Cherish Editions by visiting cherisheditions.com or by joining us on:
Twitter @cherisheditions
Facebook @cherisheditions
Instagram @cherisheditions

You can also find out more about the work Shaw Mind do by visiting their website: shawmind.org or joining them on:
Twitter @Shaw_Mind
Facebook @shawmindUK

Your Local Mental Health & Wellbeing Charity